John Calvin, Reformer for the 21st Century

William Stacy Johnson

WESTMINSTER
JOHN KNOX PRESS
LOUISVILLE • KENTUCKY

First edition
Published by Westminster John Knox Press
Louisville, Kentucky

09 10 11 12 13 14 15 16 17 18—10 9 8 7 6 5 4 3 2

Book design by Sharon Adams
Cover design by designpointinc.com

Library of Congress Cataloging-in-Publication Data

Johnson, William Stacy.
    John Calvin, Reformer for the 21st century / William Stacy Johnson.
        p. cm.
    ISBN 978-0-664-23408-9 (alk. paper)
    1. Calvin, Jean, 1509–1564.   2. Reformed Church—Doctrines.   I. Title.
    BX9418.J713   2009
    284'.2092—dc22

                                                                    2009001924

PRINTED IN THE UNITED STATES OF AMERICA

For Carson, Paige, Libby, and Buck

Contents

Preface: Why Calvin?

*I*n order to commemorate the five hundredth anniversary of Calvin's birth, I offer a fresh introduction to the sixteenth-century reformer for a general audience. I argue that the best way to appropriate Calvin's legacy is to recapture the reforming spirit that guided all his work. Accordingly, I have included a set of reflections in each chapter entitled "Always Reforming." These rest on the premise that the Reformed tradition is not merely a collection of beliefs from the past. Rather, it sets before us a continuing conversation and challenge. The type of reform Calvin envisioned is all-encompassing and ongoing, embracing the lives of individuals, the organization of the church, and the structures and tasks of society and politics.

This dynamic character of Calvin's movement means that being truly "Reformed" today is more than a matter of merely repeating what Calvin said five hundred years ago. We need to appreciate Calvin on his own terms. But we also need to be empowered to argue and differ with him.

For at least a hundred years historians and theologians have argued and differed with one another about how best to read Calvin. Historians have rightly insisted that Calvin be read with careful attention to his historical context. Though I am not a historian, I strongly agree with this insistence on historical awareness. As a theologian, I want to insist that this is important not only for the sake of history but for the sake of theology. For example, remembering that Calvin lived his life as a religious exile makes a difference in how we read his often misunderstood doctrine of predestination. Similarly, knowing how much Calvin desired to see the reform movement take root in his native France is crucial to interpreting his views of the church, its mission, its relationship to politics, and so forth. Historians have often accused theologians of reading their own agendas into Calvin's work and ignoring his concerns. There is some truth to this. At the same time, Calvin is more than a figure from history. His life and work have had a continuing impact through the centuries—not only on the church but on society in general. The task of the theologian is to take the measure of Calvin's contribution for new generations. That is my primary concern in these pages. I try to do so in ways that are both historically aware and theologically illuminating.

Being true to Calvin's context has required me to paint certain contrasts between Calvin and his opponents. For example, on a number of occasions I present differences between Calvin and Roman Catholicism. This is necessary to understand Calvin, but it is not always productive for theological dialogue today. Much has changed since the sixteenth century, and one of the tasks of contemporary ecumenical theology is to heal the divisions that emerged in Calvin's day. Still, differences must be understood before they can be transcended. Therefore, I have tried to err on the side of presenting Calvin and his controversies faithfully, even though I personally believe we need to move beyond the conflicts of the past.

This book is an exercise in scholarship for the church. To facilitate its use by general readers, I have minimized the number of footnotes. References to Calvin's great work, *The Institutes of the Christian Religion*, are provided in parentheses. A bibliographical section at the end provides references to works that have influenced my reading of Calvin and that readers desiring to go deeper will find useful. Study questions facilitate the use of the book in various educational contexts.

I offer this book with a sense of indebtedness to many people and institutions, far too numerous to name, who have instilled in me an appreciation for both the possibilities and the limitations of Calvin and Reformed Christianity. A few deserve special mention. I thank my friend Wallace Alston for his constant support and for his witness to a version of Reformed theology that, despite all obstacles, seeks justice and vitally engages society. I thank my editor, Donald K. McKim, for his expertise in helping me conceive of this project and bring it to completion. Above all, I thank my wife, Louise, whose encouragement, support, and help have made this book far better than it otherwise would have been.

I dedicate this book with much love to our children: Carson, Paige, Libby, and Buck, hoping that the best parts of the Reformed and reforming spirit will guide them in the years ahead.

William Stacy Johnson
Princeton, New Jersey

Chapter 1

Calvin

His Life and Influence

*M*ost of us know Calvin not as a man but as a set of doctrines. This is a shame. Calvin is too complex and interesting to be reduced to an abstract theological system. True, Calvin was a brilliant scholar. But he was also a pastor of the word of the world, a theologian par excellence, biblical commentator, preacher, debater, and, to a certain extent, even an international diplomat.

In short, Calvin was a man much more interested in being faithful *to God* than in creating or following the dictates of a rigid theological system. To be faithful to God requires an always fresh, always open, always curious engagement with who God is and what God calls us to be and do. Did Calvin have strong theological convictions? He did. Could he sometimes be difficult and unbending? He could. But he was also absolutely convinced that God alone is Lord of the conscience, and that God alone calls people in each and every generation to bear witness to the light God has given them.

Over time, Calvin's approach to Christianity came to be known as "Reformed." What does "being Reformed" mean? In Calvin's day, people struggled to provide a definition, because it was not always easy for the average person to follow the heady debates among theologians. Once Elizabeth I, that no-nonsense queen of England, was pressed to explain the difference between Calvin and Luther. The queen noted that the followers of Luther wanted reform, but the followers of Calvin were "even more reformed."

This push to be "even more reformed" is the hallmark of the Reformed tradition. The best way to appropriate Calvin for today is to focus on what this business of "being Reformed" means—to ask ourselves how God is at work reforming both church and society today.

To put it another way, it is a mistake to limit "the Reformed tradition" to a set of beliefs from the past. Following Calvin does not mean repeating every detail of Calvin's thought. What we need to recapture and imitate is Calvin's reforming spirit—his willingness to follow God—even if that means believing and following God in new ways.

In order to understand Calvin, we first need to appreciate the many facets of Calvin's career as a reformer. Once we know him better, we may begin to see why Calvin mattered then—and still does.[1]

The Young Calvin (1509–1532)

John Calvin was born in 1509, the same year that Michelangelo was painting the Sistine Chapel. He died in 1564, the year that Shakespeare was born. He was a product, in other words, of the Renaissance.

But Calvin was also a major figure in the sixteenth-century Protestant Reformation. Given the complexity of those times, we should perhaps speak of many "reformations" rather than a single "reformation." Be that as it may, Calvin was a second-generation reformer, following in the footsteps of Martin Luther. He was eight years old in 1517 when Luther posted his Ninety-five Theses, the event that launched the Protestant critique of the Roman Catholic Church.

Calvin's contribution was not to generate the ideas of the Reformation but to organize them, make them compelling, and embody them in practical life. Although Calvin was by temperament and training a scholar, he also became an accomplished politician and statesman. The strength of his personality was just as important and powerful as the force of his biblical and theological reflections.

Calvin was born into a modest but respectable family in the town of Noyon, located in the region of Picardy, in the north of France. Calvin's mother, Jeanne, died when he was around five or six years old. Calvin's father, Gérard, remarried soon after Jeanne's death.

As a boy, Calvin was sent away to be educated in the family home of local nobility. When Calvin was twelve, his father obtained a paid chaplaincy for his son in the Noyon Cathedral. Much as college scholarships do today, the stipend from this chaplaincy enabled young John to leave Noyon for the University of Paris, initially to train for the priesthood. There Calvin was immersed in the study of the liberal arts, and eventually became proficient in Latin, Greek, and Hebrew.

In September of 1528, Gérard Calvin fell into trouble with church authorities and was excommunicated. This meant that Gérard was refused the sacrament of Communion, a public and humiliating form of spiritual exclusion. Consequently, entering the priesthood became a more problematic option for young John. So Gérard directed his son to study law. Since Paris did not have a law faculty, Calvin enrolled at the University of Orléans in north-central France. There he came to be considered a virtual peer of the faculty and was awarded a doctoral degree. He continued his legal studies at the Academy of Bourges, studying with one of the most famous legal scholars of the day. Later in life, Calvin's legal training was to give him tremendous credibility in pursuing his agenda of reform.

In 1531 Calvin's father died at the age of seventy-seven. Because Gérard was still out of favor with the church, his family had to pull strings to allow him a church burial. Although Calvin never had a warm relationship with his father, he had always obeyed him. Now, with his father's death, Calvin acquired a new freedom to set his own course in life.

Being such an accomplished intellectual, Calvin found it only natural to return to Paris, where he had contacts with some of the leading thinkers of the day. He became close friends with Guillaume Budé, the lawyer and close advisor to the king of France. Contacts such as these demonstrate Calvin's stature with influential people in Paris. In April of 1532 Calvin published his first book, a scholarly commentary on a treatise by the Roman Stoic Seneca entitled *De clementia* (*On Clemency*).

Reformation Ideas Take Root (1532–1535)

The process by which Calvin became committed to Reformation ideas is somewhat obscure. Apparently, Calvin's mind was changed gradually. In any event, All Saints' Day in 1533 was a turning point. Calvin's close friend, Nicolas Cop, was being installed as rector of the University of Paris. Cop used the occasion to deliver an inaugural address that was woven full of Reformation themes, such as salvation by grace. This was a rather bold move, since eleven years earlier a monk had been burned at the stake in Paris for putting forward similar ideas. The faculty's response to Cop's speech was to charge him with heresy, and a few weeks later he fled to Basel. Some believe that Calvin had a hand in writing the speech, since his room was ransacked by Parisian authorities. From that day forward, Calvin's days of safety in Paris were numbered.

For a year Calvin wandered from place to place, finding refuge with wealthy friends and pursuing his studies as best he could. In the meantime, Reformation sentiment continued to build in Paris. On October 19, 1534, in a single night, a flurry of printed placards rejecting the Catholic Mass appeared all over Paris and in four other cities. A placard even ended up mysteriously on the outer door of the bedchamber of the king. With the Affair of the Placards the personal safety of reform-minded scholars like Calvin was at risk. Indeed, a close friend of Calvin was arrested and later burned at the stake.

In January of 1535, Calvin left France and sought refuge in the Swiss city of Basel, where sixty-nine-year-old Erasmus (1466–1536), the greatest humanist scholar of the age, still lived. It was in the intellectual stimulation of Basel that Calvin wrote the book that would forever change his destiny, *The Institutes of the Christian Religion*. Published in 1536, this book was a response to attacks on Reformation beliefs. Calvin boldly defended the cause of the Protestants, summarizing Reformation views with simplicity and power. Not only did Calvin defend these views, but he wrote a preface to the work addressed to Francis I, the king of France. Calvin's hope was not only to persuade ordinary people but to change the political situation through convincing the monarch.

He never succeeded in convincing the king, but the publication of the *Institutes* would immediately establish Calvin's reputation as one of the leading religious minds of his day. The book was profoundly successful. Within a year of its appearance the first edition would completely sell out.

The Making of a Reformer (1536–1541)

After the publication of the *Institutes*, Calvin decided to move to the then German city of Strassburg (now Strasbourg, part of modern-day

France). Why Strassburg? It was a reform-minded city. Calvin had already spent some time there and knew its Reformation leader, Martin Bucer. It was the city where Johannes Gutenberg had invented the printing press in 1440. At the time, it boasted the tallest building in the world. It would have been an exciting place for a young intellectual like Calvin. But Calvin's life took a different turn.

Geneva: A Calling from God? (1536–1538)

As a prelude to journeying to Strassburg, Calvin took advantage of an announced amnesty and returned quietly to France to settle his affairs. It was a time of war, and armies were on the move. As he left France for Strassburg, it became clear that in order to bypass troop movement, Calvin needed to take a roundabout route. He stopped in Geneva, a city of about ten thousand inhabitants located between two mountain ranges in the region where modern day France, Switzerland, and Germany come together. Its strategic location made it a kind of buffer zone between the major political powers of the day. Calvin's intention was to stay there for only a single night.

However, a friend recognized Calvin in the local inn and immediately rushed out to find Guillaume (William) Farel (1489–1565) and tell him that the author of the *Institutes* had just arrived in town. A powerful evangelist with fiery red hair, Farel had been leading the cause of reform in Geneva and was in need of help. Interpreting Calvin's presence as a providential gift from God, Farel burst into Calvin's room and insisted that he remain in Geneva to work beside him in the cause of reform.

At first Calvin refused. He was not a practical reformer, he protested, but a scholar. He preferred a life of books, research, and academic pursuits. A bit angered by this impudence, Farel shot back that if Calvin refused and retired to his bookish self-indulgence, then God might see fit to curse him.

Calvin was shaken by Farel's words. In the sixteenth century, talk of curses and divine judgment was something people took seriously. In addition, Farel was twenty-one years Calvin's elder and spoke with authority. In the end, Calvin agreed to join Farel in the hard work ahead.

Even though he had written a major work in theology and was a celebrity in the scholarly world, Calvin was a complete unknown to the city council of Geneva. His intellect and proficiency with Scripture gained Calvin an appointment as a Bible teacher. However, the council minutes refer to Calvin simply as "that Frenchman."

Looking back on his life, Calvin remarked that when he first came to Geneva there was plenty of preaching but not yet a reformation. This is an illuminating comment. Though he had little experience as an activist, it soon became clear that Calvin was not just about talk but about action. Reform meant more than agreeing with certain lofty ideas; it had to do with the transformation of life. Together Calvin and Farel put forward new laws concerning public morals, wrote a confession of faith to be endorsed by all city inhabitants, drafted a catechism for teaching the young, and sought greater control over who was admitted to (and excluded from) the sacraments.

Shortly after his appointment, in October of 1536, Calvin attended a public disputation (an open religious debate) in the nearby city of Lausanne. At issue was whether this city too would join the reform movement. Calvin dazzled all present with his knowledge of Scripture, the church fathers, and the art of debating. It quickly became clear that Calvin had few intellectual equals.

For eighteen months Calvin and Farel worked together, but suddenly things began to fall apart. Many of Geneva's influential citizens balked at the extent of the reforms. Then a dispute arose about Communion. Geneva had a political alliance with the city of Bern and wanted the ministers of Geneva to write their Communion services according to Bernese practices. Calvin and Farel refused to compromise with the authorities. Very shortly thereafter, the two were banished from the city.

Calvin packed up his books and left in a pouring rain. His initial encounter with Geneva left him embittered. Little did he know that his relationship with the fickle city had only just begun.

Strassburg: Years of Contentment (1538–1541)

From 1538 to 1541 Calvin lived and worked in Strassburg, the place he had intended to go all along. By all accounts his years in Strassburg were the happiest of Calvin's life. Interestingly, Farel's challenge remained with him, for he did not retreat into pure scholarship. Though never officially ordained, Calvin became the pastor of a congregation of French refugees. He learned much from the Protestant leader there, Martin Bucer, about how to organize a church. He made many friends and often had persons living in his home. He also published significant works, including a commentary on Paul's Letter to the Romans and an expanded edition of the *Institutes*.

In Strassburg Calvin also got married. Finding a suitable marriage partner was a difficult task for Calvin, who was finicky and often in ill health. Though he was brilliant, even Calvin's greatest admirers knew it would be a challenge to find a love connection for their sometimes gloomy and difficult friend. A number of attempts to play matchmaker failed. In a letter to Farel, Calvin spoke of his requirements in a bride: "I am not one of those insane lovers . . . smitten at first sight with a fine figure. The only sort of beauty that attracts me is someone who is chaste, not too nice or fastidious, economical, patient and someone who will . . . be concerned with my health."[2] However, with the encouragement of Bucer, Calvin managed to contract a marriage with Idelette de Bure. She was a widow, several years his senior, who had three children. The two were married on August 1, 1540, by Farel, who marveled that Calvin's bride turned out to be pretty. By all accounts Calvin and Idelette were very happy in Strassburg.

Geneva: The Calling Reasserts Itself (1541)

In the meantime the political winds had shifted in Geneva. The city was having trouble keeping its ministers. After some struggle, a group came to power that had a good opinion of Calvin. In 1539 Calvin had published an articulate reply to a Catholic cardinal, Jacopo Sadoleto (1477–1547), who had written the city of Geneva imploring it to return to the Catholic faith. Though at the time Calvin was still smarting from the city's rejection of him, his defense of Geneva's Reformed faith was uncompromising. Not only did it become well known across Europe, it caught the eye of many of Geneva's most prominent citizens. The city urged Calvin to return.

Although Calvin neither trusted nor much liked the Genevans, he eventually decided to continue the work he and Farel had started. As if to underscore the sense of continuity, when Calvin resumed his position as a Bible teacher on September 13, 1541, he began teaching from the very verse with which he had left off in 1538.

It is often alleged that Calvin established a "theocracy" in Geneva, a form of government in which religious powers ruled supreme. This was not the case. There were very clear lines drawn between earthly and ecclesial power. The city was governed by secular magistrates. For many years, Calvin did not even have voting rights in the city. As is true of ministers to this day, his power derived mainly from his gift of persuasion.

From the moment Calvin returned to Geneva, his top priority was to reorganize the Genevan church according to the things he had learned from Bucer in Strassburg. He drafted a constitution for the church, the *Ecclesiastical Ordinances*, which became a blueprint for doing things "decently and in order." One of the key components of Calvin's church order was the creation of the consistory in 1542. This was a governing council for the church, originally consisting of nine clergy and twelve lay elders, which oversaw the spiritual and moral discipline of the community. The consistory was the spiritual and organizational predecessor to modern-day church governing bodies, such as sessions, presbyteries, and the like.

The strength of the consistory was its potential to reshape the character of a people, to create a Christian citizenry. The danger was its tendency to become an overzealous organ of social control. Some of the native-born Genevans began to resent the consistory's influence. Much of this resentment was directed personally at Calvin. Who was he, a mere French immigrant, to tell native-born Genevan citizens what to do? Social resistance increased. One man composed songs lampooning Calvin. Another feigned a coughing fit during one of Calvin's sermons. Still another publically cursed Calvin. For spite, some people even named their dogs "Calvin."

Turbulence and Triumph in Geneva (1542–1555)

Calvin preached and lectured almost every day. For the first fourteen years after Calvin's return to Geneva, his personal life was beset by various tragedies and challenges. Idelette gave birth to a son who died in infancy. Then Idelette herself fell into a long illness and died in 1549, leaving Calvin to raise three children from her previous marriage.

On the professional front, controversies raged around who had the ultimate power of excommunication, the city council or the consistory. This was similar to the dispute that had sent Farel and Calvin packing years earlier. As in the case of Calvin's father, being barred from Communion was a powerful form of social exclusion. Calvin insisted that this power should reside with the consistory, but the city council did not agree. The council's effort to overrule the consistory provoked a showdown between the ministers and the government. In the middle of the controversy, Calvin preached a sermon that he thought might be his last. But in the end, the government backed down.

In addition, political tensions between Calvin and the native Genevans worsened. One prominent Genevan who had once supported Calvin became alienated when his mother was hauled up before the consistory for insulting Calvin. To make matters worse, the same man's wife was then disciplined by the consistory for the offense of dancing. Calvin's opponents organized themselves as the "Citizens of Geneva," and by 1553 forces hostile to Calvin had risen to political power in the city.

During this time the Spanish physician Michael Servetus suddenly showed up in Geneva. Servetus was considered a heretic by the leaders of both Catholic and Protestant cities. After a dramatic trial, Servetus was burned at the stake. The death of Servetus has long been considered a stain against Calvin's record. We shall return to this episode in more detail in chapter 11.

In 1555 Calvin's long struggle with the citizens of Geneva reached a climax in which Calvin finally triumphed. Because of intensifying persecutions in France, a flood of refugees had begun to find their way to Geneva. Many of these fleeing French families were persons of some reputation and means, and this was a time when Geneva was badly in need of funds. Desiring to fill the city coffers, the council was eager, in effect, to sell the status of "bourgeoisie" to many of these refugees. The bourgeoisie had the power to vote but not to hold office, for only those born and baptized in Geneva were full citizens. Still, the right of the French refugees to vote turned out to Calvin's advantage, since most of them were entirely sympathetic to their fellow Frenchman's cause. This led to an election in 1555 when politicians favorable to Calvin were swept into office. From then on, Calvin's power base in Geneva was secure.

Final Years and Death (1556–1564)

With his triumph in Geneva, Calvin was able to turn his attention to solidifying the reform and expanding his influence internationally. Calvin carried on a voluminous diplomatic correspondence all across Europe. In these last years Calvin sent hundreds of stealth missionaries into France to help support the cause of reform. Within Geneva itself, one of the most important measures in his last years was the establishment in 1559 of the Geneva Academy, a predecessor to what today is the University of Geneva. In Calvin's day the Academy trained both children and university students. From its opening the Academy enjoyed great academic prestige and boasted a significant enrollment. It became a seedbed for Reformed ministers throughout Europe and provided a solid intellectual base for Reformed theology.

Also in 1559 Calvin published the final edition of the *Institutes*, and in that same year the city finally granted Calvin himself the status of bourgeoisie with full voting privileges. Yet in 1559 Calvin's health took a decided turn for the worse. Throughout his life, Calvin's illnesses were many: chronic indigestion, migraine headaches, chronic gout in his feet, fevers, kidney stones, possible tuberculosis, and, to add insult to injury, hemorrhoids. Calvin died, probably of an infection, on May 27, 1564. A few weeks prior to that he had gathered the ministers of Geneva together to say goodbye. At his own request, Calvin was buried in an unmarked grave.

Always Reforming: The Difference Calvin Makes

What prompts a person to become a reformer? What enables him or her to envision and effect change? There is no universal answer. In Calvin's case it was the stern word of Farel that had the effect of taking a young man bent on other pursuits and, as Calvin himself would later put it, "thrusting him into the game."

Once energized to be a reformer, Calvin devoted his whole life tirelessly to making church and society "even more reformed." Not even his many illnesses could stop him from his life's calling.

Was Calvin perfect? No. He had many blind spots. In addition to the burning of Servetus, Calvin also followed his age in believing in the burning of witches. The scientific age was about to be born, but Calvin's attention was directed to other things. Calvin's contemporary, Nicolaus Copernicus (1473–1543), was arguing that the earth revolves around the sun, but Calvin did not accept these new ideas.

Nevertheless, even Calvin's limitations are instructive. They teach us that reform is never a once-and-for-all achievement but is always an ongoing task. Calvin's failures help us see that no thinker, not even one as brilliant as Calvin, can be followed without revision or change. Calvin knew that human judgment is always subject to error. Thus the last thing he would want us to do is to adhere to something called "Calvinism." Rather, Calvin would want us to remain true to the God to whom he was ever seeking to bear witness, the God in whom all error is judged and all truth comes to light.

Calvin Time Line

1509	Born at Noyon in Picardy to Gérard and Jeanne.
1521	Appointed chaplain.
1523	Left city to study in Paris.
1528 30	Father excommunicated, and Calvin goes to Orléans to study law until 1530.
1531	Father dies. Calvin returns to Bourges and Orléans, and then to Paris.
1532	Publishes commentary on Seneca's *De clementia*.
1532–34	At some point Calvin becomes committed to the Reform movement.
1534	Nicolas Cop rectoral address. Calvin flees Paris, finding refuge with friends. In May of 1534 he renounces his income from the church.
1535	Calvin flees France and settles in the Swiss city of Basel.
1536	First edition of *Institutes*. Calvin arrives in Geneva; agrees to work with Farel.
1538	Calvin and Farel banished from Geneva.
1538–41	In Strassburg with Martin Bucer. Marries Idelette de Bure.
1541	Returns to Geneva.

1542	Organizes the consistory.
1549	Idelette dies.
1553	Burning of Servetus.
1555	Turning point in reform of Geneva.
1559	Final edition of *Institutes*.
1564	Death.

Questions for Discussion

1. Name some instances when Calvin's life took unexpected (providential?) turns. How do we discern God's leading in our lives? Where do you turn for guidance when you are at a crossroad in your own life?
2. Why did his many setbacks not stop Calvin from being a reformer? How does adversity and hardship change a person? How might personal and professional difficulties challenge or strengthen one's faith in God?
3. Why were religious convictions in Calvin's day so important that people would risk their lives to stand up for them?
4. Which of Calvin's character traits are most admirable? Which are less so?
5. What does preaching have to do with the rest of life? How would Calvin answer this question?

Chapter 2

Calvin's Vision of God

"God is known where humanity is cared for."
Calvin (Commentary on Jer. 22:16)

Calvin opens his famous book, the *Institutes of the Christian Religion*, with the following sentence: "Nearly all the wisdom we possess, that is to say, true and proper wisdom, consists of two parts: the knowledge of God and of ourselves" (1.1.1). This intimate link between knowledge of God and of ourselves is important. It means that the only authentic way to know ourselves is to be in relationship to God. It also means that knowing God enables us to see ourselves as we truly are. In short, Calvin presents the divine-human relationship as a portrait in intimacy.

Nevertheless, intimacy with God is hard to maintain in the face of massive suffering and injustice. Warfare, genocide, famine, ecological threats, and more all prompt us to cry out with the psalmist, "How long, O Lord?"

For centuries this has been the cry of God's people in the face of injustice or pain. It was often Calvin's own cry when he beheld the evils of this world. According to those present, this was even the cry Calvin lifted up from his deathbed in 1564.

What we make of this cry depends on how we envision God and God's relationship to the world. We gain a clue about Calvin's vision of God in his commentary on Habakkuk.[1] The prophet uttered a version of that same cry when he asked how long the poor would continue to be oppressed (Hab. 1:2). Commenting on another "how long" passage in Habakkuk 2:6, Calvin noted that whenever and wherever

13

human beings cry out for justice, a miracle occurs: our cries become, in a certain sense, the very cries of God.

What a remarkable image! When we cry, God cries out with us. God is present with us in our times of distress. This view of a compassionate and responsive God in solidarity with human suffering provides the best lens through which to understand Calvin's theology. Calvin is typically accused of portraying God as an all-powerful and arbitrary despot. This is an unfair caricature. This stern depiction derives, in part, from reactions against Calvin's most unpopular doctrine, the doctrine of predestination, which will be covered in depth in chapter 5. Briefly, the doctrine of predestination teaches that while humans have wills with which to make life choices, it is ultimately God who controls the final destiny of each one of us. Similarly, the doctrine of providence teaches that there is no event in human history in which God is not at work bringing correction, restoration, healing, or redemption. What we need to recognize is that Calvin intends predestination, providence, and other similar doctrines as a message of reassurance and comfort, an answer to the cry, "How long?"

The Character of the Triune God

For Calvin, God is not a concept, a "what." Nor is God a force, an "it." Instead, God is a personal and passionate "who." It is not enough to believe in God. We must recognize and trust in God as *our* God. To put it another way, we need to get to know the character of God. When we do, we can begin to put our faith and trust in God's grace.

To have faith, Calvin insisted, is to nurture a "firm and certain knowledge *of God's benevolence* toward us" in Christ, as revealed by the Spirit (*Inst.* 3.2.7). Benevolence was a major category for Calvin. Benevolence is a disposition to do good, an inclination to perform kind and charitable acts. Not only is God benevolent, but we are called to be like God and to imitate this divine inclination to goodness. If God heeds the cries of the wounded, so should we.

In his sermons and commentaries Calvin often spoke of the need to show mercy to others in response to God's grace. Human beings are created in God's image, so a violation against one's neighbor is a violation against God's own image. For example, in commenting on Genesis 9:6–7, a passage in which God explains that murder of a human being constitutes the destruction of the divine image, Calvin makes the bold declaration that "no one can be injurious to their brother or sister without wounding God."

The idea that God can be "wounded" may be a bit startling, especially coming from Calvin. After all, isn't Calvin the one whose God is supposed to be unmovable and all-powerful, an indifferent tyrant? This language of God being "wounded" signals Calvin's conviction that God has a genuine stake in what happens in the earthly arena, that God is genuinely involved in human life. God is not just some celestial spectator.

How does Calvin know this? The short answer is that God is the triune God: Father, Son, and Spirit, the God who has reached out to embrace the human condition in Jesus Christ by the Spirit's power.[2] For Calvin, it is only through this divine reaching out that we can know God. That is, we are not capable of knowing God in the abstract, God's pure "essence." But then how is it that human beings are able to experience a God who by definition transcends our experience? To make sense of this, Calvin explained that God has chosen to "accommodate" or adjust to our human capacities. Accommodation is one of Calvin's most important teachings about God.[3] The idea is that God reveals to us who God is in thoroughly human ways. God's essence exceeds human language, and yet strangely God uses human language as an accommodation to our limits. God's essence is unknowable, but paradoxically God has become known to us in Jesus Christ by the Spirit's power.

The doctrine of the triune God, therefore, becomes a complex way of identifying who God is in the gracious act of salvation. First, Calvin frequently spoke about God as Father following Jesus' practice of calling God "Abba, Father" (Mark 14:36; cf. Rom. 8:15; Gal. 4:6). Calvin's writings are full of references to God's fatherly goodness. This did not mean that Calvin thought God was literally male—remember Calvin's conviction that we cannot know God in God's essence. But he believed that we can trust that God exercises parental care for God's children. In this regard, Calvin sometimes uses motherly images for God when the Scriptures lead him in that direction. For example, in Job and Isaiah Calvin recognizes that there is biblical language describing God as a mother or nurse. For Calvin, then, we are God's children who are cared for by our divine fatherly/motherly parent.

Second, God's parenthood is all the more relevant to us because of our union with our elder brother, Jesus Christ. Union with Christ is a major theme in Calvin's theology. This union is made possible because of the Word made flesh (John 1:14). God in Christ assumes our human nature and becomes one with us. The full significance of this was first set forth at the Council of Nicaea in 325 CE. This council responded to a bishop named Arius, who claimed that the Word made flesh in Jesus was a created rather than an eternal Word. Arius could not imagine that Jesus Christ was anything other than human. So he argued that in Jesus Christ we confront the highest and best of creatures, but a creature nonetheless. The Council of Nicaea said no to Arius, a verdict with which Calvin fully agreed. Over against Arius, Calvin held that Jesus Christ was of the same reality as God the Father (*homoousion to patri*). In Jesus Christ we encounter true God from true God, meaning that Jesus Christ is God's fullest and most perfect revelation. To put it another way, in Jesus Christ God has shared God's own self with us, completely identifying with all that it means to be human. This comes from God alone, who takes the initiative to reach out to us by offering us God's own self.

Third, because of the power of the Holy Spirit at work in us, there is movement not just from God to us, but also from us toward God. Through our union with Christ, God's Spirit has engendered faith in us and made possible our adoption as children of God. Adoption is a teaching found in a number of places in the New Testament (Rom. 8:15, 23; 9:4; Gal. 4:5; Eph. 1:5). As is the case today, adoption is not something that children achieve for themselves. It is made possible by the gracious love and acceptance of adoptive parents. In the same way, Calvin taught that our adoption as God's children is completely dependent on God's gracious love. Our response to God's free gift of grace is faith, which brings with it thankful obedience to God—our way of offering ourselves to God.

So then, when we cry out to God, we encounter a God who has become one with our cries in Jesus Christ, and who seeks to redeem our distress in the power of the Spirit, being present with us in "sighs too deep for words" (Rom. 8:26).

God's Ordering, Providing, and Caring for the World

Our cries to God are pointless if God is incapable of a response. Calvin was a firm believer in God's providential care for the world.[4] Calvin considered the providence of God to be of a "watchful, effective, active sort, engaged in ceaseless activity." Calvin's view of God's providential authority was in keeping with the psalmist's declaration that the God who watches over Israel "neither slumbers nor sleeps" (Ps. 121:4), as well as Jesus' assurance that God numbers the hairs of our heads and takes care of the least sparrow (Matt. 10:29–30; 6:26).

Modern people tend to talk about God's providence as though God were somehow barging in or intervening in the world. But this is not the way Calvin understood God's caring presence in the world. This world, after all, belongs to God. It is no more an intervention for God to take care of the world than it would be for you or me to enter our own house. To speak of divine intervention suggests more of a distance between God and the world than Calvin entertained. For Calvin, God's activity is appropriate, immediate, and constant. As Calvin put it, we are always "doing business" with God.

What sort of divine activity are we talking about? Calvin distinguished three ways in which God provides for the world. First, there is a *universal* providence, which God exercises over all creation, consisting of the order of nature that governs and guides all creatures. We all live according to the rhythms of day and night and conform to the cycles of winter, spring, summer, and fall. When we eat food, our bodies automatically digest it and make life-giving energy. Calvin believed that God is at work in all these natural processes. Similarly, there are natural limits that govern our lives. If we ignore them, things will go badly. Stay out in the sun too long, and you will be blistered. Attempt to grab a poisonous snake, and you will pay the price. Go without sleep for too long, and it will affect your health. These are all general ways that God governs the world.

Second, Calvin speaks of *historical* providence. God is at work in history, in culture, and in the workings of society to bend the will of human beings to serve God's goodness. Yet the way God does this is complex. Contrary to what his critics claim, Calvin did not envision God's providence as if God were a puppeteer and humans were puppets whose every move was determined by God. For example, one metaphor Calvin invokes to describe God's interaction with us is that of a rider trying to tame a wild horse. God is the rider who remains in control, but the horse never ceases to exercise its own willfulness. God respects the integrity of our natural decision-making capacities, while working all the same to see to it that we do God's bidding.

Third and most important, Calvin imagines a *special* providence whereby God is at work in more focused and redemptive ways among the faithful. As we shall see, this lifting up of a special providence reflects a common pattern in Calvin's thought. He describes various ways in which God deals with human beings generally but then special ways that God cares for believers. According to Calvin, God is at work in all people, but God especially lives and reigns by the power of the Holy Spirit in the lives of those who believe.

In short, God is not just ordering the world according to the laws of nature, but God is also actively providing and caring for the world as well. Today few of us would agree with Calvin in attributing so much active responsibility to God in orchestrating the affairs of the world. In a post-Newtonian and post-Einsteinian world, we have different ways of thinking about the cosmos and God's relationship to it. Living as we do in a post-Holocaust age, we are less eager than Calvin to see God's hand controlling every event that transpires. We are not willing to consider Auschwitz to be the will of God.

How far does God's providence extend for Calvin? Calvin believed that nothing in this world takes place merely by chance— God is always involved. Calvin put it this way: "not a drop of rain falls, nor is any human word spoken, apart from God's will." This does not mean that God is the author of evil. There are still bad actors in the world who devise evil. Yet Calvin believed that even the designs of evildoers are ultimately controlled by God.

Some have interpreted Calvin's comments as evidence that he believed in fate. Fatalism is the view that whatever happens is bound to happen, and neither God nor human beings can change fate's course. According to a fatalistic view, human beings are besieged by uncaring powers bearing down upon them to which they must respond with gritted teeth and heroic resignation. Sometimes the Calvinist version of providence may seem quite fatalistic. But if Calvin were a true fatalist, he would not have been so active in the world for social transformation. Although Calvin was a champion of a very high view of providence, he also believed that human action plays a genuine role in world affairs. At the very least, human beings always have the option of praying to the Creator of the universe whose power operates to make all things work together for good (see chapter 5). Believing neither in fortune/chance nor fate/determinism, Calvin held that there is an intricate dance between God's will and our human will. Human beings are, to a certain extent, free moral agents, yet God still governs the affairs of the world.

A discussion of the difference between fatalism and fortune may sound overly academic to us, but for Calvin it was supremely practical. Calvin's view of providence was not forged in the classroom; it was worked out in the give-and-take of the real world. To believe in providence was to train oneself to discern the signs of the times, to look for what God is doing in the world. As a realist Calvin knew that God made the sort of world in which bad things can happen, even to good people. But Calvin was also committed to the paradox that even when things are done that violate what he called the moral "precept" of God, these same things do not have the power to thwart the will of God for the present. Even when evil happens, one needs to look for the presence and purposes of God to be at work. In other words, God's power to reconcile and redeem is far greater that the power of evil and sin to destroy.

Some have tried to soften the doctrine of providence by claiming that God merely foreknows the future, but does not decree or direct everything that happens. Calvin would have none of that. God is not a mere spectator of events from afar but is actively governing all events. Otherwise, Calvin believed, we would be without hope in the world. Similarly, Calvin rejected the claim that providence is about God granting permission for evil events to occur. Calvin considered this a distinction without a difference. If God goes so far as to permit something, then by definition God has willed it to be by allowing it to happen. Another way to put this is that when we sin, we do not catch God by surprise. Even though in Calvin's view evil things fall within God's will, God never wills bad things for their own sake. Rather, God always is at work, even in spite of sin and suffering, to bring about a greater good.

Always Reforming: Sovereignty and Suffering

Calvin's view of God's absolute sovereignty is difficult for most twenty-first-century Christians to accept. The ongoing presence of evil in the world is a stiff challenge to the view that God is directing every event in human history. Do we want to say that God orchestrated the deaths of close to six million Jews in the Holocaust? Are we content to say that when a quarter of a million people get wiped out in a tsunami, this is somehow the will of God?

Calvin had to wrestle with these same sorts of questions. He lived in a world where disease and plague claimed the lives of thousands, including many of his own close friends. It was a world in which war and death were constant. In 1545 Calvin was traumatized for weeks by the news of the utter massacre of some 3,600 Waldensian Christians, including women and children. After Calvin's death, his followers had to contend with other horrific evils. Most notable was the St. Bartholomew's Day Massacre in 1572 in which thousands of Huguenots, Calvin's followers in France, were slaughtered by Roman Catholics in the streets of Paris. The killings continued throughout the countryside for months, claiming many thousands of lives.

How long, O Lord?

Although Calvin has long been known for his unswerving belief in divine sovereignty, some of Calvin's own reflections point us toward a different way of thinking about God's power. It is interesting that the actual term "sovereignty" never appears in the *Institutes*. The term "sovereignty" comes from the political world. It connotes the exercise of raw political power. Yet the God who is revealed in Jesus Christ demonstrates a different kind of power. In Christ, God reveals who God is supremely through a person who did not possess worldly power, a crucified figure who prayed for his enemies and who forgave the perpetrators of his own death (Luke 23:34). Perhaps we do well to pay less attention to Calvin's philosophical discussions about divine providence and focus more on Calvin's preaching about the God who identified with our woundedness and who gave his life for the life of the world.

The triune God, who is our creator and redeemer, is willing to risk being wounded. More than that, this God desires to accomplish divine purposes in the world not through raw power but through building up the faithfulness of God's own people.

Calvin made an arresting observation in his commentary on Jeremiah 22:16. There the prophet Jeremiah is contrasting the wickedness of King Shallum with the righteousness of his father, King Josiah. Josiah is praised for doing justice to the poor: "he judged the cause of the poor and needy; then it was well. Is not this to know me? says the LORD." Calvin zooms in on the biblical phrase, "Is not this to know me?" This is not surprising, given that Calvin's whole theology is about knowing God and knowing ourselves. Where people fail to do justice, argued Calvin, we can be sure that they do not know God. When there is massive evil in the world, as in warfare, genocide, and global famine, it is not the doing of God, but rather the result of people who refuse to know God. In short, says Calvin, "God is known where humanity is cared for" (Commentary on Jer. 22:16).

It seems, then, that Calvin's own remarks point us to a God whose sovereignty is yoked to the sufferings of this world. For Calvin, who lived his life as an exile, belief in a God who shared our distress was a constant comfort. Responding to this God meant caring for God's people. Belief meant trusting in this God who hears our cries, this God who would rather *die* than ever abandon us.

Questions for Discussion

1. Calvin believed that we know ourselves authentically only in relationship to God, and that knowing God enables us to see ourselves as we truly are. Agree or disagree?
2. What is the difference between thinking of God as an impersonal force and thinking of God as personal and relational? What are the dangers of thinking of God in personal terms? Why does the way we envision God matter? What ways of speaking about God are most appropriate for teaching children?
3. How do you respond to the notion that God can be wounded by our sinful acts?
4. How do you understand "divine intervention?" Why do you think Calvin insisted that God is actively involved in all events, even those that are evil or that cause suffering? How would Calvin argue that God was present in catastrophic tragedies like 9/11, wars, or natural disasters?
5. Which is easier—believing in the randomness of fate or in an all-powerful God who governs the destiny of the world? Are there other options?

Chapter 3

Grace Alone, Christ Alone, Faith Alone

*L*ike all Protestants, Calvin was powerfully influenced by Martin Luther (1483–1546), the German monk turned reformer. Luther, who was twenty-six years Calvin's senior, began his career teaching Bible at the University of Wittenberg in Germany. Luther taught that we are "justified by grace through faith." This means that we are made right in God's sight not by our own action of storing up merit, but solely by the gracious action of God. Luther relied upon such passages as Romans 1:17, "For in it [the gospel] the righteousness of God is revealed through faith for faith; as it is written, 'The one who is righteous will live by faith'"; Galatians 3:11, "Now it is evident that no one is justified before God by the law; for 'The one who is righteous will live by faith'"; and Romans 3:28, "For we hold that a person is justified by faith apart from works prescribed by the law."

Luther's conviction that we are justified by grace gave rise to four Reformation mottos, three of which we will deal with in this chapter: *grace alone, Christ alone, faith alone*. A fourth, *Scripture alone*, will be the focus of chapter 4. These convictions became watchwords for reform movements all over Europe, and each was fully embraced by Calvin. But, as we shall see, Calvin also gave each idea his own unique stamp. The result was a dynamic portrait of grace. Grace is the unfolding reality of God for us, Christ with us, and the Spirit among us. Grace enables us to accept ourselves and one another and, in turn, to give our lives freely to the service of God and neighbor.

God for Us: Grace Alone

Calvin followed Luther in believing that divine grace was the answer to what both men thought was life's most important question: *How can a sinful human being come into the presence of a holy God?* This may seem like a strange question to us. There is not much in our contemporary culture that encourages us to be pure or "holy." Not many movies or TV programs have holiness as their theme. If anything, we tend to avoid people we think of as "holier than thou."

But perhaps we can grasp what was at stake in this way. Even though our society does not much honor the religious virtue of holiness, it does put a high premium on success. So did the medieval church, which argued that salvation comes from being a spiritual success, making sure to do one's best, to do everything possible to lead an exemplary moral life. The idea was that if a person simply does his or her moral best, the grace of God would step in and do the rest.[1] At first glance this may seem to be an attractive prospect. God, on this view, is in the business of rewarding us for our ethical efforts. A moment's reflection makes clear that something very similar to this theology still lives with us today. Do your best, we tell one another, and everything will be OK.

But how can we ever be sure we are doing our best? Or what if we have periods when our spiritual tanks are empty, and we are not capable of our moral best? And just how good is good *enough*? Like a person working out in a gym, we can always imagine pushing ourselves farther, faster, stronger. How can we ever live up to what God requires? Are we caught in a never-ending quest for spiritual merit and reward?

Through wrestling with Scripture, especially the Psalms and Paul's Letter to the Romans, Luther stumbled upon an earthshaking theological insight; some have referred to it as Luther's "breakthrough." Rather than obsessing over his own righteousness, Luther discovered a new sort of righteousness—the righteousness of God.

Luther's insight was simple, yet profound. What is the righteousness of God? It is of a different order than human righteousness. God's righteousness has to do with God's character. Specifically, God is absolutely trustworthy when it comes to fulfilling God's promises. Furthermore, God is faithful to us, even when we are faithless. God does this because of the excellence of who God is. Our hopes for salvation are in vain if they rest upon our own faithfulness or efforts at righteousness. Rather, our hopes rest upon the certainty of the promises of God and upon the integrity of God to be faithful to God's own Word.

That God is true to God's promises was the key feature of grace for both Luther and Calvin. God's gracious promise of salvation in Jesus Christ lies at the heart of the Christian life. The key was to take hold of that promise and believe that it is true. The guarantor of the promise is God. In this sense, the promise is external and objective to the believer. Trusting in God alone for salvation grants a deep assurance to the believer. In other words, receiving grace rests not in a merely subjective experience but in the objective promise of God, a promise guaranteed by divine actions and integrity.

This distinction has far-reaching implications. Is the church a community whose slogan is "God helps those who help themselves," or are we a community of sinners that depends on the power of God to make us into the people God created us to be in this world and citizens of heaven in the next? In other words, for Luther and Calvin it is upon God's grace alone that all of our spiritual hopes rest.

To sum it up, the motto of "grace alone" came to mean two things. On one level, it is a conviction about the way in which sinful human beings are saved: only God's favor, bestowed without regard to human merit, is able to redeem human life. On a deeper level, grace is the very definition of who God is. God is not just any old god we happen to dream up. In Jesus Christ believers know a God who is fundamentally *for* human beings.

Christ with Us: Christ Alone

Christianity makes an audacious claim. Our God is not content merely to be *for* us. If I happen to be *for* a group of people in a far-away place who are hungry and destitute, this may give them some small solace. Perhaps I can send them a letter saying, "I am for you." Yet this by itself is inadequate. What these people need is someone who is not only *for* them but *with* them as well. They need not just sentiment but solidarity. The Christian claim is that God is in solidarity with us. God was not content to remain aloof from humanity, but in Jesus Christ God determined to become one with human beings. The Word became flesh in Jesus Christ: Emmanuel, God with us (John 1:14; Matt. 1:23).

In this way "grace alone" is made real through the work of "Christ alone." The motto "Christ alone" means that only Christ can save. In the context of the sixteenth-century debates, it also meant that Christ and not the church is the mediator of salvation. It meant too that only Christ is truly righteous, and therefore in a position to save.

The righteousness of Christ, according to Reformation teaching, is to us an "alien" righteousness. It is alien in that it is external to us. It is alien, moreover, in that it is far removed from our sinfulness. Because it is to us an alien righteousness, it can only be attributed, or imputed, to us by grace. Luther sought to explain grace by analogy to a court of law. Grace is God's judicial declaration of not guilty. Even though we *are* guilty, the divine Judge declares us *not guilty*. Because of this judicial element, some have called this a forensic view of justification. Others have called it "as if" righteousness. God looks at us "as if" we possess the righteousness of Christ, even though we remain sinners.

How is it that we come to be considered righteous in Christ? We already saw in chapter 2 that the church has affirmed the divinity of Christ, considering Christ to be of the same reality as God. This was the teaching of the Council of Nicaea in 325 CE. The church's teaching about the person of Christ was given further elaboration at the Council of Chalcedon in 451 CE. There the church declared that Jesus Christ is not only fully divine but also fully human. This does not mean that Jesus is 50 percent human and 50 percent divine. Nor does it mean that some aspects of Jesus are divine and others human. Instead, the idea is that Jesus is 100 percent human and 100 percent divine. Jesus is of the same reality as God and of the same reality as human beings, except without sin.

The precise way in which Jesus is both divine and human remains a mystery. Calvin was clear that it does not happen through a mixing of the divine and human natures. Humanity and divinity remain distinct, even though each is united in the person of Christ. Yet this union does not occur in such a way, said Calvin, that the eternal divinity of God becomes, so to speak, trapped or frozen in Jesus' humanity. Even though the divine Word became incarnate in Jesus Christ, nevertheless that same divine Word is still free to rule the world.[2] In keeping with Calvin's high view of God's sovereignty, God is incarnate in Jesus Christ but also remains at work outside Jesus Christ.

Still, this high view of God did not keep Calvin from putting forward a remarkably humble view of God's work in Jesus Christ. Calvin emphasized the simple humanity of Jesus. It is by his *human* obedience that Jesus saves. This is not because Jesus was some sort of spiritual superman. Rather, just as with all other human beings, Jesus' human obedience was made possible by the power of God's Spirit. Jesus relied upon the power of God the Father, even though Jesus is the Son of God.

Calvin was vigilant in maintaining the distinction between Jesus' humanity and divinity—indeed it is one of the distinctive features of his theology. But Calvin had no problem envisioning a union between humanity and Jesus Christ. As we shall see in chapter 7, this union with Christ became a cornerstone of Calvin's understanding of the Christian life. He believed that union with Christ is not established by human efforts but only by the power of the Spirit.

Grace alone is made effective through Christ alone. When the Reformers affirmed the motto "Christ alone," they did not mean that Christ is at work apart from the broader activity of God. They understood grace to be at work in a Trinitarian way. Grace is the favor of God the Father made real in Jesus Christ and brought to bear concretely in human experience by the power of the Holy Spirit.

The Spirit among Us: Faith Alone

There is another audacious claim made by Christianity. Not only has God determined to be *for* us by being *with* us in Jesus Christ, but God is still at work *among* us by the power of the Holy Spirit. God is living out God's own life among us as we receive God by faith. Our faith is the means through which God's purposes are carried out.

The mention of faith here is important. Luther summed up the doctrine of justification in the phrase, "justification by grace through faith." Sometimes we hear people speak simply of "justification by faith." This does *not* mean that our faith activates or causes us to become justified in God's sight. To say this would be to make salvation dependent on human action; it would in essence make faith into a "work." But the idea is not that faith saves. We are made just in God's sight not by any decision or merit on our part but solely by receiving God's grace. And this grace is received through the gift of faith. An example may help here. Sound travels in waves, but unless a receiver is tuned to the frequency of the sound waves, the sound will not be picked up. God's saving grace abounds, but the only way to receive that saving grace is to have the frequency set on "faith." By adopting a posture of faith in God, we open ourselves to receive the grace that saves.

Calvin understood faith to be the work of the Holy Spirit. Indeed, the primary work of the Spirit was to unite us to Christ. This theme of union with Christ was a major one for Calvin. Because we are united to Christ, the vitality of our faith is nourished and sustained. Faith, in other words, is not just a passive virtue, rather, it is active and spiritual. It is "a firm and certain knowledge," of God's graciousness to us, which is applied to our lives in justification (*Inst.* 3.2.7). At the same time, Calvin was concerned that the Protestant church's teaching about justification had become too one-sided. To claim forgiveness through the free righteousness of Christ, apart from works, could lead one to neglect the importance of living a moral life (see chapters 7 and 8). Calvin believed that God's grace as mercy *for us* was vitally linked to God's grace as power *in us*. How do these two realities intersect?

Calvin bound these two realities together in a doctrine of double grace.[3] There is the grace by which one is *reckoned* righteous once and for all. This is the first form of grace, the forgiveness that Protestants called "justification." There is also a second form of grace by which one is *made* righteous gradually over time; this is the grace that Calvin called "sanctification." Although Christ's righteousness is an external reality that is attributed to us, we are also engrafted into Christ in an authentic spiritual union that grows internally. We not only receive the benefits of Christ but we begin to grow in grace, becoming increasingly like him. Such are the benefits of being united to Christ.

To some, these debates over justification may seem overly technical and difficult to follow. But they reflect dynamics common to all human experience. If you have ever faced extreme circumstances—a life-threatening illness, the loss of a loved one, the rigors of combat, the threat of economic disaster, or the like—then you know what it means to face limits over which you have no control. It is in overwhelming times like these that we are forced to rely on resources outside ourselves—the love and support of family and friends, the spiritual support of the church, the benevolence of relief agencies, and so on. This recognition that our help is outside ourselves can be likened to justification. The theology of justification is saying that sin and death set limits to our lives, and the only way to overcome them is by relying on a source of deliverance outside ourselves—the grace of God.

By the same token, the theology of sanctification reminds us that life always contains not only limits but also possibilities. As Reinhold Niebuhr pointed out in the mid-twentieth century, the whole of life can be seen as a tug-of-war between the need to recognize our limits (justification) and the need to actualize our possibilities (sanctification). Every situation, no matter how difficult, also contains some opportunities to act. When we act in these circumstances, we create possibilities where there were only limitations before. When we do this, we are living by sanctification. In other words, in all of life there are things we *cannot do for ourselves*, as well as things that *only we can do*. Niebuhr summed up this interplay between justification and sanctification in his famous Serenity Prayer: "God give us grace to accept with serenity the things that cannot be changed, courage to change the things that should be changed and the wisdom to distinguish the one from the other."

Always Reforming: Reclaiming the Spirit of Reformation

Through a dynamic process of biblical interpretation, the church in the sixteenth century rediscovered the message of salvation by grace. The tragedy is that the rediscovery of this message of grace led, despite the best intentions of the Reformers themselves, to a massive split between Protestants and Roman Catholics. Since then there have been numerous efforts to reach mutual understanding. Most notably, in 1999 the Lutheran and Roman Catholic Churches issued a historic "Joint Declaration on Justification." For centuries Lutherans and other Protestants have upheld the primacy of justification by grace through faith, while the Roman Catholic Church has insisted that faith must be accompanied by good works. The Joint Declaration tries to heal these divisions. One of its central affirmations seeks to balance the Protestant emphasis on justification (making us right) and the Catholic stress on sanctification (making us holy). The statement reads as follows: "Together we confess: By grace alone, in faith in Christ's saving work and not because of any merit on our part, we are accepted by God and receive the Holy Spirit, who renews our hearts while equipping and calling us to good works." This is a remarkable affirmation of Protestant and Roman Catholic unity, achieved after over four hundred years of strife.

It should be noted, however, that even in the sixteenth century when these controversies first arose, Calvin had already made a valiant effort to hold together justification (making us right) and sanctification (making us holy), as we will discuss in more detail in chapter 7. This was typical of Calvin's way of dealing with disputes. He would lift up the concerns of both sides and find a mediating solution, based on a balanced reading of Scripture.

Today people are less likely to clash over the finer points of justification and sanctification and more likely to wonder how grace relates to the reality of religious pluralism. Specifically, when we say that salvation is in "Christ alone," do we mean that persons of other religious faiths are excluded from salvation? Or is the grace of God broad enough, and the compassion of Christ deep enough, that salvation may include persons of other religious faiths? Take, for example, God's covenant with Abraham, when the patriarch was told he was being chosen to be a blessing to "all the nations of the earth" (Gen. 22:18). This argues that there is a wideness to God's mercy. Reformed Christians have always emphasized the sovereignty of God. The classical Reformed answer to the question of religious pluralism, therefore, is that God is free to determine who is saved and who is not. Almost every Reformed theologian would agree with that. Some, such as Calvin in Geneva, would hold that the number of those saved is small. Others, such as Zwingli and Bullinger in Zurich, believed that some non-Christians were surely included in the mercy of God. Even more boldly, the twentieth-century theologian Karl Barth argued that no one is excluded from the grace of God. Despite these differences, in lines attributed to Calvin, Reformed theologians of every stripe would agree:

Our hope is in no other save in Thee;
Our faith is built upon Thy promise free;
Lord, give us peace, and make us calm and sure,
That in Thy strength we evermore endure.[4]

Questions for Discussion

1. How seriously do people take their need for divine forgiveness today? Discuss the importance of the *confession of sin* and *assurance of pardon* in worship services. Do they force worshipers to take sin seriously or just the opposite?
2. What does the motto *Christ alone* mean for non-Christians?
3. What do you make of Calvin's view that faith does not save us, but rather is the way we receive salvation? If this is so, then what does save us?
4. What does it mean to "grow in grace"? What are some of the signs that a person is growing in grace?
5. Discuss Niebuhr's characterization of justification and sanctification as "limits" and "possibilities." Name some times when you have experienced life's limits and possibilities.

Chapter 4

Wellspring of Reform

Scripture Alone

*W*e have explored Calvin's life, his vision of God, and three Refor
mation convictions that guided him. We noted Calvin's belief that the
essence of God—who God is in God's innermost being—remains a
mystery to us. This doctrine that we are left only with silence
where God is concerned. Because of the good news of the gospel we
can have confidence that God is for us, Christ is with us, and the Spirit
is at work among us. But at the same time it is also accurate to say
that God remains *beyond* us.[1] God is God, and we are not. Because
God ultimately remains a mystery to us, our ways of bearing witness
to God are always partial and provisional and hence subject to the
need for correction and reform. Paul understood this when he told the
Corinthian Christians, "For now we see in a mirror, dimly, but then
we will see face to face. Now I know only in part; then I will know
fully, even as I have been fully known" (1 Cor. 13:12). For Calvin
the wellspring of this reform was constant engagement with the
Scriptures.

The Scriptures were considered by almost everyone in sixteenth-
century Europe, both Protestant and Catholic, to be inspired by God
and authoritative. The Reformers went a step further, arguing not only
that Scripture is authoritative but that it is the preeminent authority in
the church concerning all matters of faith and practice. While the
Catholic Church maintained that Scripture and church tradition were
equal authorities, the Reformers insisted on the principle of "Scripture alone."

Calvin, Scripture, and the World of Print

Calvin's first appointment in Geneva was as a teacher of Scripture. This fact is more significant than it may appear. Rightly or wrongly, being a teacher in our society is not usually thought of as a power position. But the situation in Geneva was unique. This was a city that had made a decision to reform itself, and to do so *according to Scripture*.

Thus for Calvin to be the chief interpreter of spiritual meaning in Genevan society put him in a powerful position. It meant that when Calvin spoke about Scripture, people listened and responded. Each week Calvin preached and lectured on the Bible. Not only that, but each week his lectures were transcribed for publication, meaning that his biblical interpretations influenced other Reformers all across Europe. Over his lifetime Calvin published commentaries on most of the books of the Bible. It was as a teacher of the Bible that Calvin's agenda of reform was brought to life.

What was the context in which Calvin did his interpretive work? It was very different from our situation today, and also very different from the early church. Today we take the Bible for granted. It is a book sitting there on the shelf, translated into our native tongue, with libraries full of resources to help us understand it. But this was not always so. For the first Christians there was no single book called "the Bible." In antiquity, scriptural texts existed in the form of many different scrolls. If one wanted to read, say, from the prophet Isaiah as did Jesus in Luke 4, one would locate the appropriate scroll, unroll it, and read. The very fact that different texts were physically located in different scrolls underscored the variety of biblical books and that scriptural interpretation meant dealing with distinct and separate biblical voices.

In the sixteenth century there was still some debate about which scriptural texts qualified *as Scripture*. Luther was bold enough to argue that the Epistle to the Hebrews, James, Jude, and Revelation were not of the same revelatory caliber as the other texts of the Bible. Even though most Protestants accepted the sixty-six books that now make up our Bible, they did not accept the so-called apocryphal texts that were accepted within Roman Catholicism. It was not until the mid-sixteenth century that controversies about what specific books should be included in the Bible were finally put to rest.

Not only did the final form of the Bible take shape over a long period of time, but for centuries ordinary laypeople had no access to the Bible as we know it. For one thing, manuscripts were scarce. Each was painstakingly written by hand. Prior to the Renaissance biblical texts were preserved in the form of a codex, a collection of thin pieces of wood bound together by a cord. Because each was handmade, this meant that a single book might cost several times an average person's annual income. Imagine today if an average book cost $35,000 or $70,000, or even $140,000. How many people would be buying and reading books? In addition, ordinary people in the ancient and medieval world could neither read nor write. Plus, they spoke dialects of French, or German, or Italian, while the scriptural texts existed only in the original biblical languages of Greek, Hebrew, and Aramaic or in scholarly translations into Latin. This meant that only the most educated were able to read scriptural texts.

All of this changed in 1439 when a German silversmith, Johannes Gutenberg, invented the printing press. This was the dramatic new world into which Calvin was born, as dramatic as the advent of the Internet today. Suddenly, with this new technology books could be mass-produced, at dramatically lower costs, and in the ordinary languages of the people. For the first time in world history the writings of people like Calvin could be made available swiftly to a broad audience. Without the printing press, there would have been no widely recognized and widely read book known as "the Bible." Without the printing press, there simply would have been no Reformation.

To sum it up, not only did the printing press change the way the Scriptures were presented, it also changed the way Western Christians conceived of them. Now the Scriptures were no longer a collection of individual texts, nor a single book confined to the library. Now this book, this Bible belonged to all, and interpreting its meaning became an ongoing task for laity as well as the clergy. As Luther put it so memorably, "a simple lay man armed with Scripture is to be believed above a pope or a council without it."[2]

Calvin and Biblical Authority

As noted, almost everyone in the sixteenth century agreed that the Bible had authority. The question was whether the Bible was to have preeminent authority over the traditions of the church. For Calvin and the other Protestants, this issue was clear. The church should not be exercising authority over the Bible; rather, the Bible should be exercising authority over the church.

But if we look deeper, we will see that Calvin argues the case for biblical authority in a more nuanced way.[3] Pitting the church against the Bible is a bit too simplistic. For one thing, the Bible is telling the church's story. For another thing, Calvin's view of Scripture is complex. He does not simply equate Scripture with the Word of God. Instead, he argues that the Word of God *is set before us* in Scripture (*Inst.* 1.13.7). That is, the Scriptures do not simply present the "Word of God" by their own power. Instead, they have power for us because of the authority of *the Spirit* in the church. How do we know the voice of the Spirit? We know the Spirit because the Spirit bears witness to the Word. Indeed, Calvin argued that the Bible is a dead letter to us apart from the work of the Spirit. We need the Spirit to bring the Word alive. So Calvin's more considered position seems to be that Word and Spirit *together* exercise authority in the church.

Karl Barth drew attention to this dynamic quality of Scripture in a threefold pattern he believed was consistent with Calvin. Barth noted that Reformers such as Calvin talked about the Word of God in three distinct ways: revealed, written, and proclaimed.

First, the Word *revealed* is Jesus Christ himself. Christ is God's fullest and most perfect revelation. Second, the Word of God *written* is embodied in the Scriptures. The Bible bears unique and authoritative witness to Christ, but Christ always transcends the text. Third, there is the Word of God *proclaimed*. The church continually proclaims the message of God's grace, the good news of the Word made flesh, attested to in the written Word.

Calvin's most sustained treatment of biblical authority had to do with the relationship of the Old Testament to the New. Calvin was a strong defender of the unity between the Old and New Testaments. He had no sympathy for the simplistic claim that the Old Testament offered a covenant of works, while the New Testament offered a covenant of grace. Calvin believed that God's mercy and grace were visible in both Testaments. The difference was not one of substance but of clarity.

In the Old Testament it may have been true that God's people were bound by works of the law, but they were also living in hope of a coming covenant of mercy. Similarly, the Old Testament may have spoken of "types" or "figures" of God's anointed one (messiah) such as

Israel's prophets, priests, and kings. In the New Testament, however, Jesus the Christ—God's supremely anointed One—fulfills the roles of a divinely chosen prophet, priest, and king. For these reasons Calvin maintained that in the Old Testament the Jewish people already knew Christ the mediator in their own way.

Calvin preached and wrote commentaries on almost the whole of the Old and New Testaments. In order to do this, he spent much of his life reading, rereading, studying, and wrestling with the biblical texts. Because Calvin fervently believed that the texts of both the Old and New Testaments are the Word of God written, he was convinced the Bible offers a clear message about who God is and what God would have us believe and do.

What did Calvin make of this divine message? In the previous two chapters we noted that the church views Jesus Christ as God's divine Word embodied in human form. Just as Jesus is said to be fully human and fully divine, so also Calvin approached Scripture expecting to encounter a divine message embodied in human words.

Nevertheless, Calvin did not tell us how this occurs. His comments on the nature of biblical authority were surprisingly few. Some of Calvin's interpreters claim that he considered the Bible to be authoritative because of a property it possesses, namely, being completely without error. But inerrancy is a modern, not an ancient, concept. It arose as a defense to the application of the historical-critical method to Scripture. As a widely read and dedicated scholar, Calvin was well aware of the limitations and imperfections of the biblical writers. While it is true that Calvin occasionally spoke as though God dictated the very words of Scripture to the biblical authors, this strictly metaphorical way of speaking did not mean that Calvin accepted the so-called verbal inerrancy of the Bible. In his commentaries, Calvin often mentioned the personalities, perspectives, and historical and cultural limitations of the biblical writers. He knew that there were multiple ways of dating various biblical writings. He also knew that the Bible contains occasional historical mistakes, and he had no trouble correcting biblical authors when they were in error.

If Calvin could accept that Scripture speaks a divine message cloaked in human words, then we might wonder how he would advise us to distinguish between human words and the Word of God contained in the Bible. Calvin's answer was that Scripture is "self-authenticating." This means that Scripture does not depend upon the church or other human agencies for its power or authority. Rather, through Scripture God tells us who God is. In other words, *God* is the only proper witness to God. Perhaps an illustration is in order.

Many of us are people watchers. If you are sitting in a busy airport with nothing else to do, sometimes it can be a diversion to watch strangers interact. If you have ever done this, you know that interpreting the meaning of another person's gestures and actions is not always easy. Were those tears of joy or sorrow? Was that a smile or a sneer? Was that laugh genuine, polite, or nervous? The only way to know for sure is to ask the person directly. Only then will you have clarity. Similarly, in Scripture God reveals God's own self: God's character, God's intentions for humanity, God's moral and ethical standards, and God's plan of salvation for the world. All of this is not left to guesswork but depends on the self-verifying work of God.

But can't Scripture be interpreted in many different ways? Amid the varying interpretations, how are we to discern a true word from God? Calvin's doctrinal answer was that God's Word is confirmed by the internal illumination of the Holy Spirit. The Word comes alive through the power of the Spirit, and the Spirit bears witness to the true meaning of the Word. Yet Calvin also had a more pragmatic answer. In his own commentaries, Calvin typically acknowledged more than one view of the biblical text and left it to the reader's judgment as to which was the more convincing. This is interesting. It tells us that Calvin, as a scholar, realized that biblical texts did not fall perfect and complete from the hand of God like manna from heaven. Even the understanding of God gleaned from Scripture remains partial, an understanding that must always be open to new illumination from the Holy Spirit. For now, we often see in our biblical mirror, dimly. That is why the Scriptures must be read with fresh eyes and heard with eager ears. By the Spirit's power, the biblical texts speak in different ways and communicate many layers of meaning in the life of the church.

Scripture and Other Sources of Knowledge

Calvin's motto of "Scripture alone" elevated the Bible to the primary authority in matters of faith and practice for Reformed Christians.

Yet, at the same time, Calvin also believed that we should welcome truth from wherever it arises. Indeed, in writing the *Institutes* Calvin referred to many sources of truth other than the Bible, especially classical Greek and Roman philosophers.

So then, when it comes to knowing God, what kind of truth about God did Calvin expect to be revealed through nonbiblical sources? Calvin broke knowledge of God into two parts: knowledge of God the Creator, and knowledge of God the Redeemer. Calvin believed that knowledge of God the Creator was the possession of everyone, believer and nonbeliever alike. On this point Calvin and the apostle Paul agree. Paul tells the Roman church, "For what can be known about God is plain to them [the wicked who suppress the truth], because God has shown it to them. Ever since the creation of the world his eternal power and divine nature, invisible though they are, have been understood and seen through the things he has made. So they are without excuse" (Rom. 1.19–20). Thus, knowledge of God the Creator, however vague, is also universal, because there is sufficient evidence in the natural world for everyone to recognize God as Creator of the universe, even though our human sinfulness clouds this knowledge.

By contrast, knowing God as our Redeemer—the one who saves us from sin—can be revealed only through Scripture, under the guidance of the Holy Spirit. Calvin held that to know God as Creator is important, but such knowledge alone is useless unless we also know God as our Redeemer. Only the scriptural knowledge of God as Redeemer has the power to lead us to salvation and to minister to us in our need.

But this does not mean that our natural human capacities are beside the point in knowing God and interpreting Scripture. Two internal ways of knowing God—what Calvin called the "sense of divinity" and "conscience"—are very important for him. First, the sense of divinity is an innate awareness of God's presence in one's life. Calvin believed that all people have this basic awareness. A second internal way people are in touch with God is through "conscience," a basic sense of right and wrong.[4] Calvin thought of conscience as a universal awareness of morality, part of what it means to be created in the image of God. If our sense of divinity makes us aware of God's presence and activity in general, then our conscience reminds us of our accountability to God and of divine judgment.

If it had not been for the pervasive power of original sin, Calvin thought that both the sense of divinity and conscience would have been sufficient to lead us to God—apart from Scripture. As it is, the sense of divinity and conscience operate in unbelievers to leave them without excuse before God.

Yet that does not end the matter. These two faculties, especially the moral conscience, play a special role in the lives of believer and non-believer alike. As we shall see in subsequent chapters, Calvin placed great importance on the free exercise of conscience. In defending the cause of reform, he argued that the Roman Catholic Church does not have the right to bind the consciences of Protestant dissenters. Moreover, the main purpose of reading Scripture is not merely to derive general spiritual information but also to have one's conscience stirred and instructed by the truth of the gospel.

Calvin also spoke of other ways of knowing God the Creator apart from Scripture. These were sources of knowledge external to our individual consciousness. Calvin believed that aspects of the truth of God come through nature, through the liberal arts, and through the visual and performing arts. Such knowledge also comes by witnessing God's providential guiding of history on a divinely intended course.

In short, wherever a person looks—*within*, to an innate awareness of God and to one's sense of right and wrong; or *without,* to evidences of God in nature, human history, education, and the arts—one can find the presence and power of God. These points led Calvin to conclude that *everyone* has adequate reason to know there is a God. The real question was *what kind* of God? Is God for us or against us, active or passive, kind or vengeful, gracious or indifferent, changing or constant, present or distant? Does God listen to us when we cry?

In order to answer these questions, that is, in order know what kind of God we are invited to worship and serve, we must return to God's own testimony in Scripture. There we learn that our God is one who hears the cries of the wounded and attends to the sufferings of God's people.

Always Reforming: Scripture and Subversion

It may be hard for us to comprehend today, but putting forward new interpretations of Scripture in the sixteenth century was a potentially subversive act. Under certain circumstances, it could easily get one arrested. It could even get one killed, which is why Calvin was forced to spend his life as a political exile. To offer biblical interpretations that challenged the power of the church was, in effect, to lay an ax to the root of the whole of Western culture. In a society where bishops wielded enormous power, in a culture where most people thought that the celebration of the Mass put one directly in touch with God, arguing that the Bible does not support the consecration of bishops or that it rejects the theology of the Mass was nothing short of revolutionary. If doctrines this basic could be challenged, then what was next?

Today we tend to associate a strong view of the authority of Scripture with fundamentalist, Bible-thumping preachers who reject the insights of science and culture and insist on the truth of scriptural statements despite all evidence to the contrary. Appealing to the Bible in this way operates to uphold the status quo. In the sixteenth century, the opposite was the case. Appealing directly to the Bible was revolutionary.

As we seek to understand Calvin, we forget that we presently inhabit a world where religion has become a matter of private opinion and where religious beliefs may be expressed freely with very little consequence. In the sixteenth century, by contrast, biblical interpretations had a public significance. It was a world where religion functioned to shore up the political order. So it is easy to see why some monarchs acted quickly to squelch new views of biblical meaning. By the same token, in regions that had decided to reject the power of the Catholic monarchs, such as Geneva, what better way to pursue the hoped-for reform than by appealing to the authority of the Bible, Western culture's preeminent sacred text?

Yet even for Reformed faith, Scripture alone never meant that the Bible is the sole source for theological reflection. Human knowledge is complex and derives from sources other than sacred texts alone. It would be impossible to speak intelligently about physics, engineering, nuclear power, space travel, economics, computer science, psychology, human sexuality, genetics, or any host of other topics by referring to the Bible alone. In reading Scripture we are not required to ignore the natural or social sciences or to neglect the lessons of practical human experience. Instead, belief in Scripture alone means that Scripture remains what Calvin called the "spectacles," or the corrective lens, through which we perceive the living God. Its authority derives from its ability to be our guide in matters of Christian faith and practice. It is a collection of sacred texts *about* faith, written by *those who had faith*, in order to *engender that same faith* in generations yet to come. When we expect the Bible to be a science text or a historical record or a blueprint for predicting the future, then, at best we cease to respect it for what it is. At worst we misuse it or even abuse its power by forcing it to serve alien purposes.

Because it is to the person and work of God that Scripture points, biblical interpretation is dynamic in nature. This is the reason that Reformed Christians read the Bible again and again, week in and week out. This is the reason that it is possible to hear many different perspectives in sermons drawn from the same biblical text. If the meaning of the Bible is frozen and not dynamic and changing, pulsing with new life, then there would be no need for us to continue to interpret it. There would be no need to continue listening with discernment. All we would need to do is find the one biblical scholar with the single definitive view.

But that cannot be right. Are we meant to be content with Calvin's readings and to ignore Martin Luther King Jr.'s? Are we meant to hear the voices of men who have preached for centuries and turn a deaf ear to the preaching of women?

It is time to put aside the notion that the Bible is a book for people trying to keep the world from changing. When Calvin read the Bible, the earth shook. And it still does.

Questions for Discussion

1. What do you make of Karl Barth's threefold understanding of the Word of God as *revealed* (incarnate in Jesus Christ), *written* (in the Scriptures), and *proclaimed* (in the teaching and preaching ministry of the church)? Which of these has the highest authority for believers? Why?
2. How would you respond to a person who says, "I don't believe that the God revealed in the Old Testament is the same God that is revealed in the New Testament." How would Calvin respond?
3. How do you reconcile the fact that Calvin had a very high view of Scripture (a divine message cloaked in human words) with his acknowledgment that the Bible contains errors?

4. How do you respond to Calvin's arguments that everyone has sufficient reason to know that there is a God who is Creator of the universe? Does everyone have a conscience?
5. How does the same biblical text generate multiple interpretations? How do we know which are correct? Can more than one interpretation be illuminating for the church?

Chapter 5

Chosen and Called

Election and Predestination

*M*any of Calvin's contemporary followers seem embarrassed by his doctrine of election and predestination. While the doctrine of election poses difficulties, it would be a mistake to give up on it altogether.[1] Election is not just a Calvinist teaching; it is a profoundly biblical teaching. In Scripture God elects Abraham and his offspring and calls them to be a blessing to all nations (Gen. 12:3). God chooses other individuals, such as kings, priests, and prophets, to embody divine purposes. In the New Testament Jesus Christ is frequently spoken of as God's elected one (e.g., Luke 9:35; 23:35; Acts 3:20; 1 Pet. 1:20; 2:4, 6; Eph. 1:9–10; Rev. 13:8).

Belief in election is in many ways a logical extension of the Reformation belief in grace alone. Election teaches that each of our lives is rooted in the gracious will and intentionality of God. In other words, election is meant to be a practical doctrine that gives us encouragement and hope. It is not meant to become a matter of speculative debate.

Let us remember that Calvin was living his life as an exile cut off from his native land. Election provided him the comfort that no matter what befell him, his life was secure in the grace of God. Election includes the affirmation that, prior to any action or merit on our part, God knows us, God saves us, and God empowers us for service.

God Knows Us

The doctrine of election seeks to give an answer to some of life's most important questions: Why was I born as this particular person with

42

these particular gifts? What is my purpose in life? What am I supposed to be and do on this planet?

One way to approach these questions (very popular today) is that everything, including our own birth and death, is random and arbitrary, with no underlying meaning or purpose. Our lives are a biological accident. Once we pass on our DNA, our deaths make little difference to the species, the ecosphere, or the cosmos.

Calvin offered a different answer. He was convinced that our individuality, who we are—our gifts and our calling—reside deep within the intentionality of God. Election teaches that before we were, God was; that God thought of us and called us into being; that God knows us by name; and that God has chosen to give us a future and a hope.

Some believe that this doctrine presents God as distant and aloof. In Scripture, however, the language of election is one of intimacy. To be elected by God means that God has taken special notice of us. Thus the Bible says that God sets God's heart upon Israel (Hos. 11:8). The people of God are God's treasured possession (Exod. 19:5–6). Sometimes Scripture even uses verbs to speak of God's election that are synonymous with physical attraction (e.g., Hos. 2:16–20).

One of the hallmarks of Calvin's theology is that knowledge of God and knowledge of ourselves are closely linked. On the one hand, election tells us something quite profound about the character of God. It tells us that God has determined to be *for* us. It tells us that God does not merely create us and leave us to our own devices; rather God has a special place for each of us in God's very own heart. On the other hand, this tells us something equally important about ourselves: we are loved and accepted by our heavenly Parent. It communicates that we are called to be God's people and to live in relationship to God all our days. It reminds us that we were made to live out God's purposes in the world. Since God's purpose is to love us, it suggests that our purpose is not only to love God but to love one another.

God Saves Us

To be known by God is deeply significant. But Calvin's doctrine of election and predestination is saying much more than this. Not only does God know us by name, but election tells us that God is at work in our lives to reconcile and redeem us. Wherever we go, God has gone ahead of us. God has made provision for our salvation in advance.

In saying that God sees to our salvation in advance, we need to clarify what this means and what this does not mean. Election and predestination are *not* predeterminism. Predeterminism is the idea that God is orchestrating every event in our future so as to eliminate our free will. If something has been predetermined, then it means that all choice has been eliminated; all future plans are under the control of someone else. Predeterminism assumes that we are puppets on God's strings, with no free agency at all. This was not what Calvin meant by either election or predestination, though there are times when Calvin's followers seemed to confuse predestination and predeterminism. We may believe in God's election without falling into the pit of predeterminism. In other words, being chosen by God does not require us to forfeit our freedom of will.

What does it mean to say that in predestination God has given us a destiny ahead of time? It means that we have not been thrown into the world and left to our own devices. God accompanies us but does so in a way that respects the integrity of who we are. For us to be given something by God does not deny that we are agents with free will, but just the opposite. It means that God loves us enough to entrust us with good things, and to point us to the future God has so reliably secured for us. The New Testament letter of 1 Peter compares our future hope to an inheritance that is waiting for a beloved child. God has set before us our heavenly destiny, if we will but live into it:

> Blessed be the God and Father of our Lord Jesus Christ! By his great mercy he has given us a new birth into a living hope through the resurrection of Jesus Christ from the dead, and into an inheritance that is imperishable, undefiled, and unfading, kept in heaven for you, who are being protected by the power of God through faith for a salvation ready to be revealed in the last time. (1 Pet. 1:3–5)

Election teaches that God lays hold of us and does for us what we cannot do for ourselves, namely, we are "being protected by the power of God through faith for a salvation ready to be revealed in the last time." Election offers assurance that no person chosen by God will ultimately perish. Rather, the salvation of the elect is so certain, according to Calvin, that "even if the whole fabric of the world were to fall apart" the assurance of salvation would rest secure.

But what about those who are not among the elect, the unsaved? In Calvin's day they were known as the "reprobate." We know that God is ultimately responsible for the salvation of the elect. But who is responsible for the destiny of the reprobate? Calvin's answer was that reprobate persons are justly punished because they freely choose to engage in sin of their own accord. Yet it is also God who ordains that they remain without hope. Many have felt this is unfair. Why does God offer grace to the elect but leave the reprobate lost and without hope? While we may want to challenge his teaching about the non-elect, Calvin reminds us that, by definition, God's dealings with all human beings are always loving and just.

God Empowers Us

Calvin never believed that human salvation was an end in itself. We are saved not only for our own sakes but also in order to give gratitude and glory to God. In speaking of election, therefore, it is not enough to realize that God knows us and saves us. Election includes the strong conviction that God has chosen us and empowered us to live a different kind of life for the sake of the world.

To say that God empowers us is to recognize that the effects of election are still ongoing. God may have elected us before the foundation of the world, but the working out of our salvation is not yet complete. The poet Maya Angelou expresses her amazement at people who boast that they are saved, who think that their growth in grace stops with their profession of faith, or who are confident in their status as Christians. "You are a Christian?" she asks. "Already?"[2] The truth is that we are being empowered each and every day by our election *to become* increasingly Christian.

Some are tempted to view election as though it were a special status or spiritual rank, an honored position of privilege. But for Calvin God calls us not to a special power, privilege, or prestige, but to a special service. To be chosen is to be called to live for God and others. To answer God's call is to experience a powerful sense of moral purpose.

Calvin's teaching on election had far-reaching practical implications for the life of ordinary laypeople in the church. In the medieval church it was thought that only celibate monks were carrying out a true Christian vocation. This meant that ordinary people were somehow living a second-class Christian existence. But Protestants like Calvin linked their teaching about election with the claim that people in *all* occupations in life can live out an authentic Christian vocation. According to Calvin, God assigns each person a sentry post in the world. "From this [calling] will arise the singular consolation: that no task will be so sordid and base, provided you obey your calling in it, that it will not shine and be reckoned very precious in God's sight" (*Inst.* 3.10.6). According to Calvin, whatever a person does can be done to the glory of God.

Empowered for Freedom

The empowerment of election is also connected with the gift of freedom. To be empowered by God is to be made free and responsible human beings. It may seem strange to think of Calvin as a theologian of freedom, especially since his emphasis was on *God's* activity in election. We might rightfully wonder what place this leaves for human freedom in Calvin's thought. Yet freedom was extremely important to Calvin. The first edition of the *Institutes* built to a climactic chapter on freedom. This topic of freedom will arise at several points in our discussion of Calvin, but two points need to be made here.

First, true freedom is the freedom to be what we were created to be. Human beings are made in the image of God, and so Calvin believed that anything that distorts that image is sin, which is not freedom but enslavement. Freedom, therefore, is a freedom for obedience. True freedom happens when we are *freed from sin* enabling us to be *free for service to God and others*. Put another way, the empowerment of election means that the yes we experience from God is meant to be given away to others. Through the consolation of election, together with the future it projects for us, God empowers us to embody God's yes in behalf of others.

Second, because we are created by our Creator to be free ourselves, it is incumbent upon us not to bind the freedom of conscience of others. Why is freedom of conscience so important to Calvin? To ride roughshod over the conscience of another is ultimately an encroachment upon God's prerogative. God alone has preeminent claim over the consciences of human beings. This means that our consciences should be shaped by the values and priorities of God and not by those who would distract us from God, including those in authority over us, our government, or even the church. A modern example may help here. A criminal court judge may personally oppose the death penalty, yet preside in a state that imposes it. Freedom of conscience allows for that judge to remain in opposition to the death penalty, so long as in the exercise of judicial duty he or she abides by the laws of the state.

The point is an important one: people are created with God-given powers of perception and discernment. Their opinions, judgments, and decisions matter. There is even a sense in which people's decision-making power is sacred. God's decision to elect us in Jesus Christ, then, means that our own decisions matter significantly to God.

Weighing God's Yes and God's No

Calvin is famous (or infamous) for his doctrine of so-called double predestination. This is the belief that there is a "double decree" whereby God foreordains a gracious yes to some and a horrifying no to others. That is, before the foundation of the world, God ordained some people to eternal life and others to eternal damnation.

The first thing that needs to be said is that Calvin did not invent this doctrine. He inherited it from Augustine and based it on his reading of Scripture. Many sixteenth-century Reformers accepted some version of the doctrine of election, including Luther, Bucer, and others. The second thing to be noted is that the Reformed tradition has not been unanimous on double predestination. For example, the Reformed theologian Heinrich Bullinger in Zurich preached a single predestination to eternal life. God positively decrees salvation, but God does not explicitly ordain the disastrous fate of the damned.

Yet for Calvin single predestination seemed illogical. If God decreed salvation for some, Calvin reasoned, this must mean that God decreed damnation for others. Any other view seemed to leave the fate of the reprobate to chance, which Calvin believed challenged the absolute sovereignty of God.

Today many of Calvin's admirers, myself included, have abandoned the doctrine of double predestination. The twentieth-century Swiss theologian Karl Barth so disagreed with Calvin that he completely rewrote the doctrine of double predestination. Barth agreed with Calvin that we indeed inhabit a world in which yeses and nos need to be sorted out. But Barth argued that this does not mean that God calls and cares for some and rejects others. Instead, God has reached out to say yes to *all* human beings in Jesus Christ (see Eph. 1:3–4). This singular and potent yes, argued Barth, constitutes the true biblical doctrine of election. It is not that God is bound to some and unbound from others. In the biblical doctrine of predestination, God is bound to each one of us by being bound to Jesus Christ in his life, death, and resurrection. God says yes to all by absorbing all the terrible nos of this world into God's very own heart through the suffering of Christ. In Jesus Christ God suffers the effects of sin, including condemnation (Rom. 8:1), in order to redeem the world. God saves us and empowers us in a way that is costly to God and liberating to us.

Always Reforming: Thinking with Calvin and Beyond

We may wonder how Calvin could have believed such a thing as double predestination. Yet many people today have no trouble at all believing in a secular form of double predestination. We live in a world in which some are economically "predestined" to enjoy lives of affluence and personal ease, while others have to endure lives of poverty, violence, and hopelessness. At least twenty-four thousand people a day die of starvation and malnutrition. Economically speaking, some experience life as a resounding yes, while others must struggle with what looks like a harsh and unrelenting no.

I say this not to defend Calvin. I have never found his doctrine of double predestination persuasive. But it is sobering to step back and recognize the secular forms of double predestination that dominate the globe. If one of the goals of "always being reformed" is to remind us of our own blind spots, then the doctrine of double predestination does that in unexpected ways.

For those of us who stand within the various Reformed traditions, it is important to remember that Calvin's way was not the only way.

Barth's reinterpretation of Calvin was not completely new in the twentieth century. There had always been people who dissented from double predestination among the Swiss Reformed tradition reaching all the back to that other famous Reformed theologian from Zurich, Huldrych Zwingli. Zwingli emphasized God's goodness above God's glory, and so he expected salvation to include Socrates and many others outside the Christian fold. This view of God's saving grace strikes me as a more generous and hence a more Christian vision than that given to us by double predestination. Bullinger's idea that there is a single predestination to life remains a viable Reformed option.

We also need to be mindful that our theology shapes our ethics, and ethics shapes our life together. Any vision of how God works in the world has potential social consequences. The vision that double predestination paints in which some are included and others excluded by an arbitrary divine order tempts us to view some as "insiders" and others "outsiders," some as loved by God and others not. When we do this, we need to remember that Calvin himself called double predestination a "horrible decree." Why is it that the Puritans in seventeenth-century England found it possible to contemplate the massacre of the Indian tribes in King Philip's War? Black theologian James Cone is right when he insists that "what we do to one another, we do to ourselves." To dehumanize others is to dehumanize ourselves. It is all the more revolting when we are helped in our dehumanization by invoking particular understandings of Christian doctrine.

In its truest form, the doctrine of election was supposed to point us in a different direction. Election proclaims not only that our individual lives can make a difference to God, but that God's people are blessed to be a blessing for all the nations of the earth. The upshot of election is ethics. Our lives, and how we live them, can actually make a difference to God. If we say it reverently, it seems that even God has something vital at stake in who we are and how we live. It makes a difference to God what we do, what happens to us, and how we treat one another.

Questions for Discussion

1. How does the doctrine of divine election address or answer the following questions: why was I born as the particular individual

that I am, with my specific personality and gifts? Is there any plan or purpose to life?

2. What about divine election is reassuring or comforting? What about it is difficult or disturbing? Does God "elect" to be gracious to all people or only to some? How do you account for those who will not be saved? Who bears responsibility for the unsaved?

3. How do God's love and God's justice work simultaneously? Name some human examples where both love and justice operate.

4. For Calvin, election means that God calls us not to power, privilege, or prestige but to service of God and neighbor. How have you seen this dynamic work in your own life or that of others?

5. What do you make of the fact that not all Reformed theologians agree about the finer points of election and salvation?

Chapter 6

The Workings of Sin and Salvation

Calvin's theology is about the good news of God's saving grace. In this chapter we explore one of the central features of that good news, namely, how in Jesus Christ the God of majesty comes to embrace the weakness, frailty, and brokenness of our humanity in order to redeem it.

Because of his emphasis on the depths of human sinfulness or human depravity, Calvin is sometimes accused of being a sour and severe theologian. People do not enjoy being reminded of their weaknesses and failings. Yet Calvin never expressed an interest in dwelling on sin for its own sake. In fact, his discussion of sin in the *Institutes* is relatively brief. It fits within his broader claim that knowledge of God and knowledge of self are intimately linked. A true knowledge of ourselves, he insists, must include knowing ourselves as sinners. This, in turn, leads us to place confidence not in our own capacities but rather in God.

The Power of Sin

Human beings were created good. In the opening verses of Genesis, God looks upon all creation, including human beings, and declares it all to be good (Gen. 1:10, 12, 18, 21, 25, 31). According to Calvin, the first human beings, Adam and Eve, were living in a state of "original righteousness" before they sinned.

Because of their sin, however, this original righteousness was utterly lost and human beings were left by God to wallow in a state of corruption. This brought about a new situation, in which "all have sinned and fall short of the glory of God" (Rom. 3:23). By our own doing then, "original sin" replaced original righteousness.

What are the ramifications of "original sin"? Like most Western Christians, Calvin had learned the doctrine of original sin by reading Augustine. A review of Augustine will go a long way toward understanding Calvin.

For our purposes, Augustine taught two main things about original sin. First, because of the sin of Adam and Eve, all subsequent human beings have inherited the "taint" of sin. In other words, we not only sin, but we have all inherited the *condition* of sinfulness. This means that even before any conscious sinful act on our part, we are already caught up and implicated in sin.

Second, as if inheriting the condition of sin were not bad enough, we have also inherited the *guilt* for our first parents' sin. We may be inclined to think this is unfair. Why should the children be held accountable for the sins of their ancestors? Yet in the Bible this sort of accountability is frequent. In biblical religion, sin is understood in terms of collective responsibility. For example, when Isaiah receives his call from God, he confesses not only that he is a man of unclean lips but that he dwells among a people of unclean lips (Isa. 6:5). So powerful is sin's reach, according to Augustine, that not even infants have escaped its power, its consequences—and its guilt.

One idea Augustine taught that Calvin rejected was that this inherited guilt is passed on from generation to generation through the act of sexual intercourse. Calvin held, instead, that the stain of sin gets passed on through the interconnectedness of human community. A modern image might be that our children are born into a society where there is air pollution. They did not cause this problem, but they suffer from it and contribute to it nonetheless.

For Calvin our utter sinfulness underscores our desperate need of God. Some later Calvinists have called this Calvin's doctrine of "total depravity." Yet the doctrine of total depravity was more the creation of Calvin's successors. Calvin's own views were much more ambiguous. Calvin's claim was not that human beings are so sinful that they become totally incapable of good works. Calvin is clear that good works can be done by Christians and non-Christians alike.

If for Calvin sin is "total," it is total in that it affects the whole person—heart, mind, body, and soul. It is emphatically not "total," if we mean that doing good has become impossible. For Calvin the effects of sin are total *in extent*—the whole of life has been infected with sin. However, the effects of sin are not total *in degree*—we have not been turned into completely diabolical beings.

Calvin's hardcore account of sin led him into a realistic view of life. While Calvin knew that not every manifestation of sin appears in every person, he also knew that under the right circumstances each of us is capable of the worst sins imaginable.

Calvin's view of sin also led him to develop a complex view of free will, a view that his followers have puzzled over for generations. He had no doubt that human beings have freedom of choice; the question is whether we have the freedom to act unencumbered by the influence of sin. For Calvin sin permeates even our best thoughts and actions, which is why we so desperately stand in need of redemption by a power outside ourselves.

Freedom of the Will

Calvin is often accused of creating a doctrine of sin that de-emphasizes freedom of the will. But this applies more to some of Calvin's followers than to Calvin himself. For example Calvin seems to admit that the will can resist God, even though later Calvinists made the irresistibleness of God's grace a hallmark of their theology. In order to understand Calvin's teaching about the will, we need to pay attention to four key points.[1]

First, Calvin affirms that we always have *freedom of choice*. This is the simple power to do this or that. Even sinners subsequent to the fall retain the power to choose certain simple actions. I have the power to throw my pencil into the wastebasket or not. I can decide to go to the market this afternoon or tomorrow. According to Calvin, we have never lost this rudimentary aspect of free will when it comes to "earthly things." Yet when it comes to "heavenly things"—the things that pertain to God and to the spiritual life—our freedom is presently in the grip of sin.

This leads us to the second aspect of freedom, an aspect that has been lost due to the fall: the *freedom to do what is good*. In Romans Paul said, "I do not do what I want, but I do the very thing I hate"

(Rom. 7:15). Paul went on to lament, "nothing good dwells within me, that is, in my flesh. I can will what is right, but I cannot do it" (7:18). New Testament scholars still debate what Paul meant here, but Calvin and his followers believed it was Paul's autobiographical confession of the ongoing power of sin to thwart even one's own best intentions. In short, the question is not whether we can do the good we will; the question is whether we can will to do the good. Note the paradox here. Calvin did not deny freedom of the will; he denied the *purity* of the will.

This leads to a third point: *the necessity of the will*. This notion is based on the assumption that what we choose to do *necessarily* reveals who we are. Thus the will can be thought of as the character of a person put into action. This is all well and good until you recall that the fundamental fact about who we are is that we are sinners. Our actions reflect our willful choices, and our actions show us to be sinners. Thus when we sin, we sin *with* our wills, not *against* our wills. This leads us into the following dilemma: if we are sinners, then our freedom of will is a problem; it inevitably causes us to sin. True freedom, in Calvin's view, is the freedom to obey God. The "freedom" to do evil is a false freedom.

Fourth, Calvin also speaks of *conversion of the will*. This is brought about by the work of divine grace. God does not bend our wills by coercion or force. Calvin says that God does not seek to "hurl us as though we were stones." Rather, God respects that we are independent creatures with free will. As previously mentioned, Calvin uses the analogy of a rider trying to tame a wild horse. God is the rider and our wills are beasts out of control. God works with us, offering both discipline and encouragement so that our obedience is not forced out of fear, but instead is offered as a loving response to God out of gratitude.

The Image of God: Lost and Restored

According to Scripture, human beings are created in the image of God (Gen. 1:26–27; 9:6). Calvin believed that being in the image of God separated human beings from the rest of creation. On the one hand, the divine image consists of natural, God-given human capacities, such as reason and freedom. On the other hand, it also includes spiritual capacities, such as worshiping and honoring God. Being in the image of God means ultimately that human beings are called to mirror God's goodness on earth.

Yet Calvin also taught that one of the awful effects of sin is that it radically distorts the image of God. Some have understood Calvin to say that the image of God is totally lost, in keeping with the idea of total depravity. Calvin does use language from time to time that leaves the impression that sin totally destroys the image of God. In some places Calvin speaks of the image having been "obliterated," "destroyed," and "wiped out." But in other places Calvin specifically says the image has not been obliterated, destroyed, or utterly wiped out. Instead, it has been seriously corrupted.

Be that as it may, that all people are created in God's image still serves as an important standard in Christian ethics. We are to respect and refrain from harming one another, because all of us are equally created in God's image. Each of us is precious in God's sight. Says Calvin: "we remember not to consider men's evil intention but to look upon the image of God in them, which cancels and effaces their transgressions, and with its beauty and dignity allures us to love and embrace them" (*Inst.* 3.7.6).

The enduring character of the image is important not only for ethics but for our understanding of God. In chapter 2 we noted that in Calvin's Genesis commentary he insisted that if we do anything to harm another human being, we are wounding God.

If we were to sum up Calvin's doctrine of humanity, it would have three elements.[2] First, we are created in the image of God. Second, the image has been distorted but not destroyed. Third, God's plan is to restore the image in human beings through Jesus Christ, the true image of God (2 Cor. 4:4; Col. 1:15).

Christ the Savior: Our Prophet, Priest, and King

The liberating power of the gospel resides in the life, death, and resurrection of Jesus Christ. This power comes from what theologians call the "person" and the "work" of Jesus Christ—both from *who he is* and *what he does*.[3] We have just discussed how Jesus Christ is the image or mirror in whose reflection we see God. Yet this role of reflecting God is one that was originally assigned to all human beings. *We* were created to reflect God, but we failed. Thereafter, Christ accomplished what we failed to accomplish. However, God has not given up on us. God still wishes for *us* to fulfill this task of being divine image bearers. Indeed, this is the goal of salvation. But in order to see how this is so, we must examine Calvin's teaching on the person and work of Christ with this ultimate goal in mind.

In speaking of the *personhood* of Christ (the "who"), Calvin affirmed the ancient belief from the early church councils that Jesus was both fully human and fully divine (see chapters 2 and 3). We noted that this meant Jesus was not 50 percent human and 50 percent divine but 100 percent human and 100 percent divine. But let us stop and think about this. To say that Jesus was fully human is to acknowledge that he experienced human frailty, that he cried over the death of his friend Lazarus (John 11:33), that he was subject to suffering and death. But it means something else too. It means that God chose to save us in a thoroughly human way, through a thoroughly human figure, who lived a thoroughly human life. To be sure, in this human life, divinity was truly embodied and made real. But this embodied divinity lived among us in complete solidarity with our humanity.

Calvin also followed, at least in broad outline, the teaching of Anselm of Canterbury that only a mediator who is both divine and human is able to reconcile humanity to God. On the one hand, Jesus needed to be human, for it was human beings whose sin had incurred an infinite debt against God. On the other hand, Jesus needed to be divine, for only the power of a divinity is able to satisfy an infinite debt. We have already explored in chapter 4 the idea of imputed ("as if") righteousness; that is, the belief that God attributes the righteousness of Christ to us, that God has declared us to be "not guilty" even though we are sinners. This acquittal from the penalty of sin is part of what Jesus does because of who Jesus is.

In stating the *work* of Christ (the "what"), Calvin offered an innovative interpretation of Scripture, setting forth Christ's threefold office of prophet, priest, and king. Calvin was not the first to write about the threefold office, but he was the first to give it a full systematic expression. It is interesting that the church has never set forth a single, definitive doctrine of the work of Christ. Rather, the church has allowed many understandings to flourish. Calvin's threefold approach offers a way to gather up a number of these aspects into a reasoned whole.

One somewhat surprising feature of this threefold designation is that it places Christ squarely within the tradition of ancient Israel, emphasizing Jesus' Jewishness in a time when the church was bent on distancing itself from the Jews. Another aspect that should now make sense to us is that all three of these offices are in every way human. It was human beings who fulfilled these roles in ancient Israel. Now it is Jesus Christ, the Word made flesh, who fulfills them all to the highest degree.

Prophet

Calvin understood Jesus Christ to fulfill the role of a prophet, because he proclaimed the truth about God and about the human condition. Jesus' teaching ministry is well attested in Scripture. Jesus also engaged in prophetic deeds, such as the cleansing of the temple (Mark 11:15, par.) and his triumphal entry into Jerusalem on a donkey (Matt. 21:1–9). Such deeds symbolically demonstrated God's judgment upon God's people but also pointed to the hope of divine deliverance.

Even though Jesus was a prophet, standing in a long line of biblical prophets, he also fulfilled this office in a unique way. He not only pointed the people of God to the truth, but he embodied divine truth in his own person. In John's Gospel Jesus says, "I am the way, and the truth, and the life. No one comes to the Father except through me" (John 14:6).

Priest

Jesus Christ also fulfilled the office of priest. In ancient Israel priests mediated between God and the people by offering sacrifices on behalf of the people to make atonement for their collective sins. This is a function Christ also fulfills, although in a more intensified way. Christ is our priestly mediator by virtue of offering up *himself* as a sacrifice. Calvin believed that by Christ's self-sacrifice he satisfied divine justice and reconciled an alienated humanity to God.

Jesus also executes the office of a priest in continually making intercession on our behalf at the right hand of God. This was an important part of Calvin's teaching. He lived in an age when the Roman Catholic Church urged people to pray for the Virgin Mary and the saints to intercede on their behalf. Calvin's conviction was that Christ alone is in a position to intercede. That Christ does intercede (John 17) should be cause for great comfort for those who believe.

King

Jesus Christ is our king, having risen from the dead and ascended into an eternal kingdom. His kingly status was already anticipated during his life, albeit in hidden ways. When he rode on a donkey into Jerusalem people hailed him as Son of David (Matt. 21:9). A sign in three languages proclaiming Jesus "King of the Jews" was nailed to the cross over his head as he was being crucified (John 19:19–20; cf. Matt. 27:37; Mark 15:26; Luke 23:38). While clearly meant to mock him, this placard created by his tormentors turned out to be a banner of truth.

In Calvin's teaching, Christ carries out the office of a king by strengthening and protecting believers and leading them to salvation. The kingly office of Christ points us to the power of his resurrection and to his authority and power to save. The Westminster Shorter Catechism summarizes Jesus' kingly role as "subduing us to himself, in ruling and defending us, and in restraining and conquering all his and our enemies" (Q.26).

Always Reforming: God's Faithfulness and Our Fragility

God renews us in God's own image through the life, death, and resurrection of Jesus Christ. In so doing, God restores us to true freedom, the freedom for obedience.

Yet there is a profound tension within this story of salvation. On the one hand, it is a story of a God who is powerful. In Calvin's perspective, God holds all the power there is (chapter 2), determines to save us by grace alone (chapter 3), and makes sure that those whom God chooses will persevere until the end (chapter 5). God is a God who takes the initiative to redeem God's people. This is a powerful narrative indeed.

On the other hand, God exercises this saving power in a thoroughly human way—embracing our weakness, fragility, and brokenness in Jesus Christ by the Spirit's power. In other words, the biblical narrative is a real narrative, with real twists and turns. Jesus is tempted in the wilderness (Matthew 4:1–11; Luke 4:1–13). Jesus is confronted by demonic powers that cause disease and threaten God's reign (e.g., Mark 1:21–28). The drama is heightened when Jesus wrestles with whether to accept his impending fate in the Garden of Gethsemane (Mark 14:32–42; Matthew 26:36–46). The stakes in the drama are brought home to us when Jesus dies (Mark 15:37, par).

Moreover, God looks for a human response on the part of those who are confronted with Jesus' story. Both Jesus' story and our story are about real events, with real risks, in which God has a real stake.

Both aspects of this narrative are important and must be affirmed—God's saving power *and* God's suffering purpose. Both the power of God and the perfection of that power through weakness are important parts of the story.

Nevertheless, some of Calvin's immediate successors had a hard time holding these two affirmations together. This became clear in the decades after Calvin's death in a controversy over the meaning of election, sin, salvation, grace, and perseverance. A Dutchman, Jacob Arminius (1560–1609), who had come to Geneva to study with Calvin's successor, Theodore Beza (1519–1605), raised questions about Calvin's strong views on election and salvation. Arminius had no problem believing in God's prevenient election; but he held that election bases itself on God's foreknowledge of a person's faith in Christ. In other words, it is ultimately having faith that saves a person. He also objected to the claim being made by many of Calvin's followers at the time that Christ died *only* for the elect. Calvin himself never put it quite this way. Calvin stated clearly that God desired that all be saved, but he also underscored that many are in fact not saved. Another claim made by the Calvinists to which Arminius objected was that God's grace is irresistible. Arminius felt it was clear, from both Scripture and experience, that some people do resist the grace of God.

At the Synod of Dordrecht, held in the Netherlands in 1618–1619, the so-called Calvinists rejected Arminius's views and summarized their own in five points, which are usually given the acronym TULIP:

1. Total depravity: human beings are so completely sinful that we are unable to contribute anything to salvation.
2. Unconditional election: election does not depend on any human response.
3. Limited atonement: Christ's death is salvific only for the elect.
4. Irresistible grace: God's grace cannot be resisted by the human will.
5. Perseverance of the saints: once saved, always saved.

The common denominator in all five is the idea that God's grace is completely invincible. These five points *must* be true, so the argument goes, because to deny any one of them would, in effect, turn God into a failure. For example, what does it mean if Christ died for all, but Christ's death fails to save all? The Calvinist's answer was that Christ's death is sufficient to save everyone, but it is effective only for the elect.

I would like to stress that Calvin himself never put forward these "five points of Calvinism." Calvin's treatment of most issues is much more subtle. Seldom is his method of argument so rationalistic; usually he relies upon his rhetorical skills and powers of persuasion. After all, if our subject matter is God, isn't some reticence called for? Is it really possible to speak about the ways of God with such surgical precision? Remember that at best we see in a mirror dimly when it comes to God.

Many of Arminius's followers were banished; some were imprisoned; one leading politician was executed. This carries with it a lesson. The Calvinist-Arminian debate, like many other theological issues, was part of a broader political conflict, in this case the struggle between the Netherlands and Roman Catholic Spain. The Dutch Calvinists represented the party that favored war; the Dutch followers of Arminius were from the party that wanted peace. Sometimes deeper struggles over power cause theological disagreements to turn ugly.

Rather than trying to resolve issues of this sort through logic, I find it best to remember that the invincible grace of God is most visible in the "foolishness" of the cross. For as Paul put it, "God's foolishness is wiser than human wisdom, and God's weakness is stronger than human strength" (1 Cor. 1:25). A theology bent on reform must always keep this in mind.

Questions for Discussion

1. For Calvin sin is not only wrongs for which we are individually responsible, but also is a condition into which we are collectively born. Consequently, even babies are subject to the power, consequences, and guilt of sin. Do you agree with this picture of human sinfulness? If not, then how is sin at work in our world?

2. Calvin's view of sin implies that under the right (or wrong) set of circumstances, each of us is capable of the worst sort of sin imaginable. How does recognizing our common sinfulness change the way we view ourselves and others? How would living out our common need for grace change the way we treat each other within the Christian community and outside it?

3. Calvin understood the human story to be a three-act play: we are created in the image of God; sin distorts but does not completely destroy the image of God in us; God's plan is to restore the image in humans by the Spirit's power through Jesus Christ, the true image of God. What about this narrative is helpful? What is not? What might need to be added?

4. Calvin agreed with Anselm that Jesus had to be truly human and truly divine in order to reconcile humanity to God. What about this way of explaining the person and work of Jesus is helpful? How do you understand Jesus' role in salvation? How would you explain this to a young person? To a non-Christian?

5. Why do you think that the church has never set forth a single, definitive doctrine of the work of Christ?

Chapter 7

Participation in God's Ways

The Power of the Spirit

*T*o twenty-first-century ears, aspects of Calvin's thought may seem overly technical and difficult to comprehend. But we should not be deceived. Calvin was a pastor who was primarily concerned with spiritual matters. This is evidenced in the personal seal he had made that depicted him freely giving his heart to God with an outstretched hand. Calvin also had a motto: "My heart to you I offer, Lord, promptly and sincerely." Calvin wanted people to experience God directly, to participate in God's ways. He even made the audacious claim that the work of Christ (a subject we considered in chapter 6) is of no use at all to us unless we have been brought into relationship with God by the power of the Holy Spirit.

How does this happen? According to Calvin, the Holy Spirit is the bond that unites us to Christ. The primary accomplishment of the Spirit is to bring us to faith.

Faith

Calvin considered faith to be the primary vehicle by which God's blessings are received. "Faith alone" was one of the mottos of the Reformation. Luther and Calvin held that salvation comes to human beings not through any act of merit on their parts but solely due to the grace of God, received by faith.

But what, specifically, is faith? Calvin offered a carefully crafted definition. Faith is the "firm and certain knowledge of God's benevolence to us, founded upon the truth of the freely given promise in

Christ, both revealed to our minds and sealed upon our hearts through the Holy Spirit" (*Inst.* 3.2.7). This definition can be broken down into several parts.

First, *faith is a form of knowledge*—not an abstract, bookish sort of knowledge but a personal knowledge similar to the way we know a close family member or a trusted friend. It is an intimate and familiar knowledge. Thus the faith Calvin is talking about is very different from "blind faith." True faith is not content merely to accept what others say without question. It trusts its own direct acquaintance with God's ways.

Second, *faith has a clear object*. One puts one's faith in God as revealed in Christ and as made alive by the power of the Spirit. For Calvin faith was not just wishful thinking; it was not just a cheery disposition in life. It was, quite specifically, faith centered in God.

Third, faith in God *focuses squarely on the character of God as gracious*. Faith is certain of God's goodness and benevolence toward us. Yet Calvin was always a realist. He recognized that this certitude does not have to be rock solid all the time. He is very clear that even weak faith is real faith. The certainty of faith rests not on some sort of personal aptitude for faithfulness but upon the believer's unity with Christ, as accomplished by the work of the Holy Spirit. Says Calvin, "Christ is not outside us but dwells within us" (*Inst.* 3.2.24).

Fourth, faith rests on the *strength of God's promises*. A promise, whether made by God or by anyone else, is a peculiar sort of utterance. It is, by definition, not yet realized—it is promised for the future. To this extent, faith is very close to hope. Hope is the expectation of things that faith has believed. The belief that God is absolutely faithful to God's own promises, according to Calvin, is the basis for all Christian faith.

Fifth, faith *involves the whole person*. Just as sin affects the whole person (see chapter 6), so also faith is complete and holistic, involving both the mind and the heart. The mind may have to be cleansed and the heart fortified in order for faith to be built up in us. Calvin often spoke disparagingly of any form of religion that was "frigid." Faith was supposed to be warm, vibrant, and alive.

Sixth, faith leads one to *assurance of salvation*. This was a major difference between Luther and Calvin, on the one hand, and the traditional theology of the Roman Catholic Church, on the other. Protestants believed it is possible to know that one is in a right relationship with God. The Catholic Church considered such assurance to be presumptuous.

Repentance, Regeneration, and Forgiveness

Calvin's emphasis upon certainty did not relieve the believer of the need to come before God in repentance. This was so important that Calvin offered another special definition. Repentance is defined as "the true turning of our life to God, a turning that arises from a pure and earnest fear of him; and it consists in the mortification of our flesh and of the old man and in the vivification of the Spirit" (*Inst.* 3.3.5). Calvin held that repentance is necessary in order to receive forgiveness from God. But repentance is not the cause of forgiveness. Why? Because forgiveness flows solely from the mercy of God. We repent not in order to gain forgiveness but because we have been forgiven.

How to unpack this definition of repentance? First, true repentance is never trivial or superficial. It entails the "true turning of our life to God." In other words, repentance must be authentic. As such, repentance is a consequence of faith. This is a foundational belief for Calvin. We would have no confidence in turning to God if we did not know God to be merciful. True faith leads one to repentance, and repentance opens the door to the transformation of the soul itself.

Second, repentance, like faith, is *connected to a full appreciation of God's character*. Calvin said repentance requires fear of God. It is aroused by a sense of divine judgment. The term "judgment" needs to be explained. To our ears it may sound like an overly harsh and condemning word. But for Calvin the *judgment* of God does not necessarily equal the *condemnation* of God. A parent may pronounce a word of judgment against the action of a child, but this does not mean that the parent condemns and rejects the child. Judgment is like shining a light in a dark room. It illumines what is there—both the good and the bad. Everyone is judged by God, but in Christ not everyone is condemned by God (Rom. 8:1).

Third, repentance is *ongoing*. Calvin did not think of repentance as an event that necessarily happens all at once, at a particular time. Calvin was not an advocate of dramatic conversion experiences. His own experience of repentance was more gradual and nonspecific. He knew that true repentance takes a lifetime.

Fourth, Calvin thought of repentance as involving *a dynamic action of putting to death and coming to life*. These two movements he calls "mortification" and "vivification," and they also are the subject of careful definitions.

For Calvin, "mortification" is a "sorrow of soul" that comes from knowing that one is a sinner who stands under divine judgment. Mortification comes from the recognition and acknowledgment of the evil in one's life. Mortification literally means putting something to death. It is a dying to sin and living to righteousness. Mortification is a putting to death of the old, God-hating, neighbor-hating, self-destructive way of living (dying to sin) and exchanging it for a life of love of God and neighbor (living unto righteousness).

This living unto righteousness Calvin called "vivification," a coming alive to Christ in the power of the Spirit. Calvin thinks of vivification as a consolation that comes specifically from having faith. Because one trusts in God through faith, one is enabled by the Spirit's power to rise up, take heart, regain courage, and return from death to life. The goal of repentance is not for us to wallow in the past. The goal, rather, is the restoration of the image of God in us that has become tarnished due to sin.

Some people think that Calvin had a tendency to overemphasize mortification. Calvin's focus on "fearing God" may contribute to this impression. Yet it is also true that in our self-indulgent culture the self-critique that mortification requires is both unpopular and rare. Even if Calvin tilted the balance toward mortification, in principle he held that dying to self and living unto God are equally important and must be interwoven with one another. It would be wrong to separate mortification from vivification and to dwell on the negative and not celebrate the joy that is ours in Christ. It would be equally wrong to move too quickly to claim spiritual victory without confronting our own failings.

Repentance and regeneration are used by Calvin as virtual synonyms for the process of sanctification. Sanctification is the process by which God makes us holy. For Calvin, sanctification and justification are linked. Indeed, through his concept of a "double grace," Calvin was one of the first theologians to help the church see the difference between justification and sanctification, but also their interconnection. Justification is the act of God's free grace by which we are accepted as righteous in God's sight based on the righteousness of Christ being attributed to us by grace. Sanctification is a corresponding act of God's free grace by which God enables us to experience regeneration, namely, to die unto sin, live unto righteousness, and be renewed in the image of Jesus Christ. Being forgiven (justification) and being renewed (sanctification) are both part of the same action of God's grace. Justification has already happened in Christ; but sanctification unfolds by the Spirit's power over the whole of one's Christian life.

It is interesting that Calvin presents his theology of sanctification, or regeneration, *before* discussing justification. Given the centrality of justification in the sixteenth-century Protestant movement, this is not what we would expect. By discussing repentance and renewal first, Calvin seemed to want to avoid any implication of "cheap grace." We can receive the gospel, in Calvin's view, only by obeying it.

Another important feature of sanctification for Calvin bears mentioning. We are all forgiven (justification), but some people grow faster, and others grow more deeply into sanctification. For example, we may all agree that Mother Teresa grew more in grace than most of the rest of us. We are all equal with Mother Teresa in receiving the benefits of justification. We are not equal in our growth in sanctification. Justification, in other words, is a one-time act that is equal in all; sanctification is an ongoing process that varies in strength from person to person.

One of the ideas introduced in chapter 3 was so-called imputed righteousness—the righteousness of Christ that is attributed to us even though we are sinners. Some have contrasted the Protestant view of imputed righteousness with the Roman Catholic Church's teaching about "imparted" righteousness—a righteousness implanted in the human being that becomes the ground of our reconciliation with God. In Calvin's understanding, however, righteousness is in a sense both imputed and imparted. Something is done *for* us once and for all, but something is also gradually done *in* us as well. In short, we are both justified and sanctified (considered righteous) now, but enabled more and more to be righteous in the future.

Yet in speaking of God doing something *in* us, Calvin was careful to maintain the distinction between divinity and humanity. Calvin rejected the ideas of some of his opponents that God's own essential righteousness somehow becomes part of our own human fabric. For Calvin it is a mistake to think that our humanity is commingled with divinity. Yet in his own way Calvin does advocate a type of human participation in the ways of God. He thought of it this way: some church fathers argued that God became human so that human beings could become like God. But Calvin modified this to claim that God became human so that human beings could become *children* of God (*Inst.* 2.8.2). In this way Calvin preserved a sharp distinction between God and humanity while also arguing for a kind of intimacy between God and humanity. This was not merely an abstract argument in Calvin's mind, for he insisted that Christ cannot be known apart from the regeneration of our hearts and our sanctification by the Spirit, nor can living the Christian life be separated from true piety or reverence toward God.

The Christian Life

The forgiveness and renewal that God wishes to bestow upon us become real for us through the concrete act of Christian living. Calvin's discussion of the particular features of the Christian life is one of the most moving in all his writings.[1] He understands the Christian life as living out our identities as children of God. Our example, of course, is Jesus Christ, which means that our lives are to be an expression of the life of Christ. Following the apostle Paul, Calvin sees this as "presenting our bodies as a living sacrifice" (Rom. 12:1). Calvin explains that the Christian life has four main features.

First, we are called to *self-denial*. Quoting Paul in 1 Corinthians 6:19, Calvin begins with the strong affirmation that we belong not to ourselves but to God.

> We are not our own: let not our reason nor our will, therefore, sway our plans and deeds. We are not our own: let us therefore not set it as our goal to seek what is expedient for us according to the flesh. We are not our own: in so far as we can, let us therefore forget ourselves and all that is ours.
>
> Conversely, we are God's: let us therefore live for him and die for him. We are God's: let his wisdom and will therefore rule all our actions. We are God's: let all parts of our life accordingly strive toward him as our only lawful goal. (*Inst.* 3.7.1)

Self-denial not only deepens our relationship with God, it leads to right relationships with our fellow human beings. A stance of self-denial leaves no room for selfishness or pride. It enables us to follow virtue for its own sake rather than for the sake of receiving praise.

Second, the Christian life entails *cross bearing*. Calvin grounds the life of cross bearing in the words and life of Jesus. Jesus died on a cross, but Calvin interprets the whole life of Jesus as a "perpetual cross." Everything about the life of Jesus led to the cross.

If we pattern our lives after the cross, we will be led to trust in God, to be patient and obedient. It will condition us to accept adversity when it comes, and so we will interpret life's difficulties as part of God's "fatherly chastisement."

Third, we are called as Christians to *meditation upon the future life*. Thinking about the blessed life that awaits us gives us a proper perspective on the present life. As we face tribulation, we will be weaned from excessive love for this life and instead look with joy to life in eternity with God. Calvin wanted us to see the present life as an exile, a prison, a sentry post until Christ comes again. He noted how strange it is that Christians fear death, when they should know that "to live is Christ and to die is gain" (Phil. 1:21).

Fourth, we are called to *the proper use of the present life*. Even though we need to keep the present life in perspective, we should always use the things of this life in a way that gives honor to God. Here Calvin advises something like "everything in moderation." We should be neither too lax nor too strict regarding the concerns of this life. In finding the right balance, each of us must rely on our conscience. The main principle, says Calvin, is to use worldly possessions in accordance with God's intention. But lest we go astray, Calvin offers us some guidelines. First, we should recognize God as the author of every good gift. Second, we should live modestly, bearing poverty peaceably and abundance moderately. Third, we must be good stewards of what God entrusts to our care, for we will be asked to render an account for them. Finally, in all these matters we should strive to live out our Christian vocation or calling.

This last point is extremely important. According to the medieval church, only a priest or a monk was actually living an authentic Christian life. Calvin strongly disagreed, maintaining that all of life's worldly occupations may be blessed by God. It is no more noble to be a lawyer or a minister (like Calvin) than to be a plumber. Calvin believed that those living in the "real world" had a calling from God. Even the humblest occupation provides opportunities to give God glory: "From this [calling] will arise also a singular consolation: that no task will be so sordid and base, provided you obey your calling in it, that it will not shine and be reckoned very precious in God's sight" (*Inst.* 3.11.6). In chapter 11 we will consider the profound implications of this conviction for society and politics.

Christian Freedom

Living in the Spirit brings with it freedom. One of Calvin's most powerful convictions is that we are enabled to be free and responsible persons in Christ, because God alone is Lord of the conscience. We already noted in chapter 2 that all people possess a conscience by which they are able to discern, however imperfectly, the claims of God upon their lives. For Calvin the freedom that conscience provides is not a freedom to do just anything. Our consciences are meant to be captive to the Word of God. This freedom that is ours in Christ has three features.

First, we have the freedom that is ours in *salvation by grace alone.* As such, being in Christ frees us from the rigors of legalism. Because we are justified not by obedience to the law but by grace through faith, we are not bound by a restrictive understanding of the law. As we shall see in chapter 8, this does not mean that we can ignore the law. But we must understand that the law is a form of the gospel. The law does not merely levy prohibitions but gives positive direction to life.

Second, we have the freedom of *responding in gratitude.* We follow God and do God's will not out of an external necessity but out of a free obedience born from within. Such freedom is impossible for people bound by sin. But with the gift of the gospel, our hearts are changed. We are in the process of being transformed, and this transformation enables us to do God's will joyfully rather than by coercion.

Third, we have *the gift of freedom of conscience regarding adiaphora ("things indifferent" or "things that do not matter").* These are things over which Christians may reasonably differ without breaking fellowship with one another. One example Calvin gave was whether to kneel in worship—it does not matter. Another was controversies over whether ministers should wear robes or not—it does not matter. Other things Calvin classified as "not mattering" had more far-reaching consequences. For example, 1 Timothy 2:11–12 says that women should keep silent in church. Calvin classified this as a teaching that was contingent on its circumstances, and thus could be changed in the future. The same was true of teachings about women's head coverings (1 Cor. 11:5).[2]

There are some things that do not matter in some contexts but that do matter in others. Let us consider an example. Should we have an American flag in the sanctuary? Arguably, it does not matter. It is an issue over which reasonable Christians may differ. However, what if the government demanded that Christians give total allegiance to the state and deny the lordship of Christ? Under such circumstances, having a flag in the sanctuary might become an act of betrayal.

Writing in an authoritarian culture, which exercised complex mechanisms of social control, Calvin's emphasis on freedom of conscience is quite remarkable. Calvin's teachings on freedom suggest that Christians sometimes have to make judgment calls about issues that are ambiguous. One of Calvin's strong theological convictions is that in Christ God has graciously adopted believers to be God's children. Calvin took quite seriously the teaching of Paul: "For you did not receive a spirit of slavery to fall back into fear, but you have received a spirit of adoption. When we cry, "Abba! Father!" it is that very Spirit bearing witness with our spirit that we are children of God, and if children, then heirs, heirs of God and joint heirs with Christ— if, in fact, we suffer with him so that we may also be glorified with him" (Rom. 8:15–17). Living into our Christian freedom means remembering that we are heirs of the living God.

Always Reforming: Living into Christian Freedom

The ramifications of Calvin's teaching on freedom of conscience are wide-ranging. Calvin's third aspect of freedom invites us all to cultivate powers of discernment, so that we can take the measure of our spiritual and cultural situation. If there are beliefs and practices in church and society that do not matter, then this invites Christians to develop a sanctified imagination. It empowers us to think beyond the limitations of any particular historical context. We have permission to envision a different sort of church, and a different sort of world, than what we see around us. It is toward this sort of reimagining that the church should devote its energy.

Moreover, Calvin's teaching about this third aspect of freedom assumes that there will be differences, and even disagreements, in the church. Disagreements are part of the normal condition of human life. We may even look upon these differences as signs of God's grace. In the midst of difference, Calvin urged Christians to be united on essential matters. Yet unity does not mean uniformity. Calvin's list of essentials was quite short. He mentioned such points as the unity of God, that Jesus is the Son of God, that salvation is by grace, that God is triune, and not much more. In his own pastoral practice, Calvin often looked for ways to compromise and to live in reconciled friendship. On occasion Calvin did not practice his own best advice. But this was a human failure within Calvin, not a failure of the principle of Christian freedom itself.

In the midst of controversy, one of Calvin's helpful bits of advice was to strive not to give offense to our Christian brothers and sisters. Calvin also warned Christians not to take offense when none was intended. In this regard, repentance and the practice of forgiveness are applicable throughout life. They call us to mutual forbearance, even when disagreements seem intractable.

In recent years, mainline Reformed churches have seen bitter controversies over a host of issues, such as biblical interpretation, the meaning of human sexuality, war and peace, and much more. In the secular arena, as well, we live in times that are full of economic, political, and geopolitical challenges. In these challenges we confront both possibilities and limits. As explained in chapter 3, understanding the interplay between the limits and possibilities of life is one of the central dynamics of Christian living. It is the challenge of living by both justification and sanctification. We live by the grace of God that accepts us as we are. But we live, too, inspired by the freedom of the gospel to strive continually to become better than we are. It is this that a Reformed church lives for.

Questions for Discussion

1. Name some ways that Calvin's understanding of faith differs from "blind faith." Why does Calvin say that even weak faith counts as real faith? Do you agree? Based on Calvin's definition of genuine faith, what would you say to someone whose faith is wavering?

2. What are the hallmarks of being in a right relationship with God? Where do you put your confidence regarding your own relationship with God?

3. Explain how repentance can be necessary in order to receive forgiveness, yet not be the *cause* of forgiveness. Why doesn't Calvin equate the judgment of God with the condemnation of God? Is repentance a process or something that happens all at once?

4. Discuss Calvin's four main features of the Christian life: *self-denial; crossbearing; meditating upon the future life; proper use of the present life.* What characteristics are central to your understanding of the Christian life? What would you eliminate? What would you add? Which gave you new insights into Christian living?

5. Reformed Christians often quote the words, "God alone is Lord of the conscience." What do these words mean? What do they *not* intend to say?

6. Calvin believed that some things truly do not matter in terms of one's relationship to God. Name some of these. Give some examples of other things that might matter in one context but not in all contexts.

Chapter 8

What Does God Require of Us?
Law and Gospel

T o be a Christian, for Calvin, had a strongly ethical edge: it was to live out the purposes of God. It stands to reason that if we seek to serve God, then we should be eager to conform to the will of God. But how do we know the will of God? One answer is through the law. The law is not just an arbitrary set of rules but an expression of God's very own character. So then we need to be immersed in the divine law, while always recognizing that the law is a form of the gospel.

The Law Is a Form of the Gospel

The law was central to Calvin's vision of the Christian life. In fact, Calvin opened his first edition of the *Institutes* with a chapter on law. But how do we square Calvin's emphasis on the importance of the law with his corresponding belief in justification by grace through faith? If we are saved by grace, then what is the role of the law? Calvin's answer was precise. Works of the law are not the *cause* of salvation, but they are the *fruit* or *hallmarks* of salvation. For Calvin the law is a vehicle through which we can experience God's goodness toward us.

Calvin rejected every form of antinomianism, the false belief that in Christ God has completely done away with the law. Instead Calvin asserted that there were three functions, or uses, of the law.

First, there is the *theological* use. The theological use of the law, said Calvin, is to help us realize our status as sinners and our resulting need for salvation. Because we cannot obey God's laws perfectly, we fall short of the moral purity that the law demands. Thus the law functions diagnostically, telling us that we are sick; we are sinners in need of salvation from outside ourselves. We see this diagnostic side of the law when we heed the radical words of Jesus in the Sermon on the Mount. There Jesus said that even to speak ill of a person placed one in danger of eternal punishment (Matt. 5:22). He also said that just looking at another person lustfully was already to have committed adultery in one's heart (5:27–28). Jesus takes the letter of the law and invites us to appreciate the intensity of its spirit: "You have heard that it was said, 'You shall love your neighbor and hate your enemy.' But I say to you, Love your enemies and pray for those who persecute you" (5:43–44). When viewed in this way, the law sets forth a standard that is beyond our reach.

Second, there is the *civil* use of the law. We have civil laws that aim to restrain evildoers in our society, whether they are Christian or not. No matter what our religious beliefs, when we are driving a car down the highway and see a police officer, we usually slam on the brakes and worry that we will be pulled over. Even if we were not speeding, our instinct is to slow down. We believe the "law" is going to condemn us. This use of the law recognizes that civil laws function to curb evil impulses and help to keep citizens in line, whether they are Christians or not.

Third, there is the *didactic* use of the law. This is the use that is most important for believers. The law not only convicts people of sin (first use) and restrains people from unrighteousness (second use), but, by grace, it gives believers positive guidance concerning the will of God for their lives. Calvin calls this third use the *principal* use of the law.

Here a contrast between Luther and Calvin is worth noting. For Luther the theological use was most prominent—the law convicts us of sin. This is why in traditional Lutheran services the Ten Commandments were sometimes read prior to the confession of sin. We hear the law, and our proper response is to confess our sin. In Reformed worship, however, the Ten Commandments were read after the confession of sin and the assurance of pardon. Having received assurance of forgiveness, the believer is strengthened by God's grace to follow God's commandments.

The Ten Commandments

The Ten Commandments have always enjoyed a place of honor in Reformed theology.[1] Calvin and later Reformed theologians divided the commandments into "two tables," a reference to the two tablets Moses carried down the mountain (Exod. 24:12). The first table (commandments one through four) have to do with one's duty to God, while the second table (commandments five through ten) focus on one's duty to neighbors. In this way the two tables were thought to reflect the commandment of Jesus to love God and neighbor (Matt. 22:35–40).

Calvin offered three rules for interpreting the Ten Commandments. First, the focus of the commandments is not just conformity to an external set of rules but inward, heartfelt obedience to God, the giver of the commandments.

This meant, second, that the commandments are more than mere words on a page. In interpreting them, we must look not simply to the *words* of each commandment but also at the *reason* that lies behind the words. Behind each negative prohibition in the law there is a positive principle or a reason. For example, we are not to murder. The prohibition is clear. But the reason that we are forbidden to murder is because life is a precious gift from God. Beyond our obligation not to murder our fellow human beings, we have the obligation to promote human welfare and flourishing—to enhance the life of others.

Third, Calvin reminded his audience that there are two different types of commandments, those pertaining to love of God and those concerned with love of neighbor, and the two are entwined. We cannot love God while hating our neighbor, and vice versa (1 John 4:20). Even though love of God should not be reduced to love of neighbor, our lives best conform to God's will when they bear fruit for our neighbor.

First Commandment

I am the LORD your God, who brought you out of the land of Egypt, out of the house of slavery; you shall have no other gods before me.
(Exod. 20:2–3)

For Calvin this was not just a negative admonition to refrain from following other gods, but it also contains the positive implication that we are to give God adoration, trust, and thanksgiving. According to Calvin the reason for this commandment is that God desires the primary allegiance of God's people. In this commandment we learn two things. First, God alone is God. This is the basic premise of monotheism, and it is a staggering premise indeed. It means that our ultimate loyalty is to God; and all other allegiances—to nation, to tribe, even to family—are subordinated to this primary commitment. Second, our God is a God who saves, a God who delivers people out of bondage.

H. Richard Niebuhr, a twentieth-century Reformed theologian, helps us see the comprehensive scope of this commandment. Niebuhr interprets it not merely as an affirmation of monotheism but of "radical monotheism."[2] It is "radical" because it judges and calls every aspect of human cultural life into question. This radical monotheism challenges every form of polytheism, the idea that there are many gods. In a certain sense our pluralistic culture bears witness to many gods, to the demands of multiple allegiances. Radical monotheism also challenges the false identification of God with the cause of one's own social or political group, culture, or nation. In true monotheism, God is recognized as the sole Creator and Redeemer of all people.

Second Commandment

You shall not make for yourself an idol, whether in the form of anything that is in heaven above, or that is on the earth beneath, or that is in the water under the earth. You shall not bow down to them or worship them; for I the LORD your God am a jealous God, punishing children for the iniquity of parents, to the third and the fourth generation of those who reject me, but showing steadfast love to the thousandth generation of those who love me and keep my commandments.

(Exod. 20:4–6)

The second commandment prohibits making or worshiping a graven image. This commandment forbids us to reduce God, who is spiritual, to an earthly form, as well as forbidding us from worshiping any such form. Calvin also points out that the commandment prohibits us from imagining God apart from Jesus Christ.

Calvin sums up the problem of idolatry in a single line. Idolatry occurs when we dare to imagine God according to our own capacities. This suggests that all our concepts and ideologies—even our theology—can slide into idolatry. To try to take the measure of God in any form is arrogant, as though it were in our purview to judge God rather than the other way around. Humanity is a "perpetual factory of idols," Calvin observed (*Inst.* 1.11.8). Much of his pastoral practice was aimed at protecting people from church practices he considered to be sheer superstition.

Third Commandment

You shall not make wrongful use of the name of the LORD your God, for the LORD will not acquit anyone who misuses his name.
(Exod. 20:7)

The reason for the rule against taking the name of God in vain is that the name of God should be considered holy, just as we pray in the Lord's Prayer, "hallowed be your name." To understand Calvin's interpretation of this commandment, it helps to know that swearing an oath in the medieval world had some serious moral consequences. Swearing was a way of sealing an obligation. The person making the oath invoked God to verify his or her sincerity. Thus God became a party to the transaction. And if God was part of the contract, then failing to fulfill it was thought to bring down divine judgment not only upon the offender but upon the whole community. In this way oaths were common ways to create social bonds, so their integrity needed to be preserved.

Standing against this practice were the Anabaptists, a religious group in the sixteenth century that refused to take oaths at all. The Anabaptists took literally Jesus' teaching in the Sermon on the Mount that one should never swear an oath (Matt. 5:33–37). Calvin rejected the Anabaptist interpretation, arguing that Jesus' warning not to swear at all meant never to swear "in vain." From this Calvin argued that it was perfectly permissible to swear an oath in a court of law, or the like—provided one swore truthfully.

Fourth Commandment

Remember the sabbath day, and keep it holy. Six days you shall labor and do all your work. But the seventh day is a sabbath to the LORD your God; you shall not do any work—you, your son or your daughter, your male or female slave, your livestock, or the alien resident in your towns.

(Exod. 20:8–10)

The keeping of this command, says Calvin, entails three things. First, the Sabbath was a time not just of rest but of "spiritual rest." It was a time to lay aside human work and "allow God to work" in us. Calvin saw this day of rest as a time to contemplate the future everlasting rest that God is preparing for us by the power of the Spirit.

Second, this day of rest was a time to assemble and worship God. It should include hearing the Word, partaking of the sacraments, and time for public and private prayer.

Third, the Sabbath had a social and political dimension. Our rest is not meant merely to be self-indulgent. But rest is to be granted all who labor, and especially those who labor as servants. The commandment even includes noncitizen aliens or immigrants. In keeping with his overall interpretive approach, Calvin understood this aspect of the commandment broadly. We should not in any way oppress or take advantage of persons who work for or perform services for us, whether on the Sabbath or any other day.

Fifth Commandment

Honor your father and your mother, so that your days may be long in the land that the LORD your God is giving you.

(Exod. 20:12)

The purpose of this commandment, said Calvin, is to encourage us to respect those whom God has placed over us. Calvin extended the same principle to submitting to political leaders, as well as respecting one's pastor. It made no difference, Calvin tells us, whether those in authority happen to be worthy or unworthy. We should honor them for the sake of their office. This honoring includes not begrudging them the salaries to which they are entitled—a word that had a special appeal to the clergy!

So far Calvin's interpretation could not be more authority-friendly. Yet Calvin went on to pair this commandment with the words in Ephesians 6:1, which he interpreted as a limitation upon the apparent command to obey authorities absolutely. In Ephesians we are told that we need only obey our parents "in the Lord." From this Calvin concluded that when parents themselves disobey the law of God, the children are within their rights to disregard their commands and even to treat them as strangers. Some people have spiritual "fathers and mothers," mentors from whom they derive more guidance than their own earthly parents. However, for all of us our ultimate allegiance should be to our heavenly Parent.

Sixth Commandment

You shall not murder.
(Exod. 20:13)

The purpose behind this commandment is to bind humankind together in social and political unity. At the most basic level, we are tied to one another because we are each created in the image of God. Since we are a part of one another, how can we even contemplate murder? To murder a neighbor is to put to death a part of our own humanity—and what is worse, to offend God by destroying a bearer of God's own image.

But we can also violate the commandment in other, more subtle ways. Merely refraining from shedding blood is not enough to fulfill this commandment, because according to the words of Jesus, even to harbor hatred of our neighbor is to violate the murder command. In order to obey this commandment fully, we must positively attend to the well-being of each of our neighbors.

Calvin noted that our obligation to seek the welfare of others is strongest toward all those to whom we are the closest—our family and friends, the neighbors near at hand, the people we know especially well. We should do good toward all people, but especially those who in God's providence are bound up most directly in our lives.

Seventh Commandment

You shall not commit adultery.
(Exod. 20:14)

The purpose of this commandment is that the purity and faithfulness of our covenant-making God are to be reflected in the covenants of our own lives. We have been created, Calvin notes, for relationships of companionship, friendship, and intimacy. The relationship of marriage to a "helper suited for us" has been blessed by God. Any sexual union outside marriage is rejected by God.

So serious a crime was adultery in the sixteenth century that those found guilty were often punished by death. Aside from his biblical insights into this matter, Calvin had to deal with adultery in his own larger family circle. Calvin's brother, Antoine, had a wife who was accused of adultery on two different occasions. The first accusation, in 1548, resulted in court-ordered reconciliation. The second, in 1556, ended in divorce. Divorce was almost never granted in medieval Europe. Annulment was granted if it could be established that a true marriage had never taken place. In those rare cases in which a divorce was granted, the divorcing parties were not allowed to remarry. Ironically the staunch position that the city of Geneva took against adultery helped open the door to divorce with permission to remarry.

Calvin also used his discussion of this commandment as an occasion to reject celibacy, with the exception of the very few who have been granted sexual abstinence as an extraordinary gift. Joining other Protestant reformers, he repudiated the Roman Catholic Church's requirement of mandatory celibacy for priests. Calvin acknowledged that sex is a biological drive that cannot be easily squelched, and so he considered it normative for most people to marry, invoking the advice of Paul that it is better to marry than to burn with lust (1 Cor. 7:9). Calvin even went a step further and argued that *not* to marry is to disobey one's calling. "If his [a man's] power to tame lust fails him, let him recognize that the Lord has now imposed the necessity of marriage upon him" (*Inst.* 2.8.43, 1:407).

Eighth Commandment

You shall not steal.
(Exod. 20:15)

The eighth commandment forbids taking what rightfully belongs to another. This commandment has as its purpose the elimination of injustice, which Calvin considered an abomination to God. Calvin also operated with the premise that people's possessions have been allotted to them as part of the providence of God. This being the case, stealing represents a direct affront to the providential will of God.

Theft can take many forms. It occurs when employees fail to do an honest day's work, or when people fail to pay their debts. It is also robbery when the powerful oppress the less powerful, even if they have the "permission" of unjust laws. People are also being short-changed when ministers do not take care of their flock or when parents do not adequately nurture their children.

This commandment is not just a negative and restrictive word, it is also a positive and expansive mandate to do justice. Not stealing includes actively working for the good and care of others. We will return to this at the end of the chapter.

Ninth Commandment

You shall not bear false witness against your neighbor.
(Exod. 20:16)

This commandment reflects God's character as a God of truth who hates lies. Each of the commandments in the second table has to do with the well-being of one's neighbor. This one speaks specifically about telling no lie concerning one's neighbor. On the surface, the prohibition against bearing false witness arises in a judicial context. We are not to tell a lie against a neighbor in court.

Nevertheless, in keeping with his general approach to the commandments, Calvin broadened it to include never saying anything that would harm one's neighbor, including not saying anything behind his or her back. We bear false witness when we engage in put-downs or when we start rumors in casual conversation. Even statements that may be true can serve to damage a person. To slander or defame a person, said Calvin, not only hurts the person but breaks the bonds of community that hold all of us together.

We might think that speaking falsely is not as bad as killing or stealing. Yet in his sermon on this commandment, Calvin maintained that telling lies about neighbors is even worse than stealing from them. It is worse because we are not just taking objects from people, but we are harming the people themselves by taking away or even destroying their reputations. In other words, character assassination is still an assassination, a killing, a death. For this reason Calvin compared speaking falsely to murder. In both cases we ignore the image of God in the persons we hurt.

Calvin also took aim at people who are too quick to point out the evils that others do. This kind of self-righteous behavior constitutes another way of violating the commandment. People who are unable to bear the faults of others will find that others will not be able to bear with them. Just as Jesus confronted sinners with grace, so also we should follow Jesus' gracious example and forbear with one another.

Tenth Commandment

> You shall not covet your neighbor's house; you shall not covet your neighbor's wife, or male or female slave, or ox, or donkey, or anything that belongs to your neighbor.
>
> (Exod. 20:17)

This commandment exists, Calvin reasoned, because God wants us to care not only for ourselves but also for our neighbors. When we view ourselves as "have-nots" and look with envy on those who "have," then strife is not far away and living as community is threatened. Calvin's view is intensified by his belief that people's possessions have been allotted by God. Hence to want more of the world's goods would be to challenge the wise providence of God. Covetousness focuses on human distinctions. Here is the vision Calvin offered instead: "we ought to embrace the whole human race without exception in a single family of love; here there is no distinction between barbarian and Greek, worthy and unworthy, friend and enemy, since all should be contemplated in God, not in themselves" (*Inst.* 2.8.55).

Always Reforming: The Law as Agent of Reform

The law was central to Calvin's vision of church and society. Perhaps this is not surprising, given Calvin's legal education. Though Calvin functioned in Geneva as a pastor, he had more legal training than anyone else in the city. This made him a formidable presence in city life. It also gave him the resources he needed to envision a societal structure built on Reformed convictions and principles.

The Reformed interest in law went far beyond Calvin's own legal preparation. Many Reformed Christians around the world have taken a keen interest in the legal and ethical institutions that are necessary to make for a more equitable and more just society.

Given this concern, it is understandable that the Ten Commandments, especially the second table, became for Calvin signposts for how society should be positively ordered. In a modern secular society such as ours, it is neither possible nor desirable to impose the literal Ten Commandments onto our legal statutes and interpretations. Nor should our common civil government become the protected territory of one religion alone or be structured in a way that denies freedom of religion to anyone, no matter what their religious convictions. Still, Christians are encouraged to carry their own convictions into the civil arena, so long as it is done in a way that contributes to the common good.

A Reformed approach to law will never be content with the world as it is, but will always be working toward the world as it ought to be. Given the insights derived from the Ten Commandments, this will be a world in which justice is pursued for all, and in which there is equality for all citizens (commandment eight). It will be a world in which the well-being of everyone is given protection and support (commandment six). It will be a world in which the integrity of relationships is respected (commandments five and seven), in which denigration of others is rejected (commandment nine). In short, it will be a world in which persons are given priority over material things (commandment ten).

Calvin considered the promotion of human welfare to be a divine priority. When God's people are hurting, it is ultimately God who most feels the pain. Consequently, when we act to alleviate human suffering, we give glory to the God who is with us in our suffering. Obedience to the Ten Commandments is not about obeying rules; it is supremely about furthering God's gracious and redemptive purposes for the world.

Questions for Discussion

1. Calvin points to three uses of the law: *theological, civil,* and *didactic.* How have each of these uses of the law played a part in your own life?
2. The following are questions arising from the various commandments. Discuss as many as you can:

   - Calvin observed that behind every negative prohibition of the Ten Commandments, there is a positive principle or reason. As you look at each commandment, name the prohibition implicit, the positive action that flows from it, and the reason for each.
   - What in our national life might lead us to conclude that we are functionally polytheistic? Where have you noticed a false identification of God with a specific cause, group, or position on an issue?
   - It is possible for all our concepts and ideologies—even our theology—to slide into idolatry. Where have you seen this happen? What can we do to prevent our dearest convictions from becoming idolatrous?
   - In what ways do we see Sabbath rest observed in our day? Violated?
   - How do you view Calvin's move to extend the honor and obedience due parents to other authority figures such as political leaders and pastors? How do you view this commandment as you think of your own parents? If you are a parent, how do you view it in relation to your own children?
   - Calvin likens "bearing false witness" against another person to murder. Why? Do you agree?

Chapter 9

The Church

Meaning, Ministry, and Mission

*I*n May of 1534, just months before his twenty-fifth birthday, Calvin made a dramatic decision. He undertook a special trip, traveling over four hundred miles on horseback, to his hometown of Noyon. There he renounced his chaplaincy and the payments he had been receiving from Noyon Cathedral. We do not know what was going on in Calvin's mind as he made this gesture. Coming as it did approximately six months after Calvin's flight from Paris and a year before he would take up residence in Basel, this renunciation seems to have been an act of integrity, marking a pivotal step in Calvin's spiritual pilgrimage.

These actions meant a clean break between Calvin and a Roman Catholic ecclesiastical system from which he was becoming increasingly estranged. Calvin never thought of himself as leaving or betraying the church that had nurtured him. If anything, that church had betrayed *him*. Rather, his goal was to revive the true meaning of the church as a spiritual fellowship—a church whose essence was to be found not in its institutional bureaucracy but in its adherence, by grace, to God's Word and Spirit.

What It Means to Be the Church

Calvin followed Martin Luther in maintaining the principle of the "spiritual priesthood of all believers." This notion of a priesthood that was not limited to clergy undermined the institutional structure of the Roman Church. This meant that God is capable of acting apart from the institutional church, an idea in opposition to the teaching of the Roman Catholic Church. However, his belief in the spiritual priesthood of all believers did not mean that Calvin thought that the church is unnecessary. Calvin had a strong view of the church's place in the Christian life. He acknowledged that believers need the church as an external "means of grace" to aid them in their spiritual journey.

Some of Calvin's opponents objected that a church whose priesthood included all believers was a church without clear lines of authority. Such a church was seen by some as too radical, for it threatened to devolve into anarchy. Yet Calvin's response was uncompromising. The only line of authority in the church is not apostolic succession but the Word of God. The church's identity is grounded in the gospel of Jesus Christ, and particularly in the gospel of justification by grace through faith. In keeping with that gospel, Calvin maintained that the church is God's creation and not a work of our own hands. The church emerges, grows, and comes to us as a gift of God's Spirit.

As his work as a reformer progressed, Calvin developed an increasingly dynamic vision of the church—a church that is simultaneously catholic, orthodox, evangelical, and reformed.[1]

The Church as Catholic

When we hear "catholic" we likely think of the Roman Catholic Church, but Calvin understood the church to be "catholic" in the sense of being a single church that is universal. This is how he interpreted the article of the Nicene Creed that held that the church is "one," "holy," "catholic," and "apostolic." The "holiness" of the church, for Calvin, consisted not in the special qualifications of its priests or leaders but in its listening to the Word of God. Because the church is populated by sinners, its holiness remains incomplete for now. The church is holy (literally "set apart") only in that it is a community that desires to be set apart *from sin* in order to be a community set apart *for God*.

The Roman Catholic Church claimed to be "apostolic" because it could boast a continuous, uninterrupted chain of priests from the apostle Peter to the present. But for Calvin the church was apostolic not because of a leadership chain from the past but because of a substantive adherence to the apostles' teaching, as witnessed to in Scripture.

Calvin could not have conceived of the reality we know as "denominations," nor could he have imagined the current relaxed church situation in which people "church shop" and often hop from one denomination to another. In the sixteenth century there was only one church in a particular region, and all people were expected to belong to the same church body as their secular ruler. In addition, Calvin would be bewildered by the lack of attention paid by most believers today to the theological distinctions over which people fought and died in his day.

The Church as Orthodox

The term "orthodox" literally means "right opinion." Calvin was certainly one who hoped the church would espouse right opinions about the gospel. Yet in the Reformed churches no pope or central authority was empowered to define right opinion. For Calvin the arbiter of such matters was simply the Word of God. Calvin maintained that the Word of God was clear and comprehensible—it did not need the pope to interpret its meaning.

Even though Calvin was a Western Christian who was seeking to reform the Roman Catholic Church, he also was immersed in the writings of the major Eastern Orthodox theologians. As we have seen, Calvin accepted the teachings of many of the early Eastern Orthodox councils, especially the Council of Nicaea (325) and the Council of Chalcedon (451), which taught that in Jesus Christ we encounter one who is both fully human and fully divine. On the other hand, Calvin did not accept the Eastern Orthodox practice of venerating icons.

We should not think of orthodoxy as something fixed or given. Seeking out right opinion about the nature of the Christian faith is an ongoing task. This should mitigate the objections from those who consider the quest for "orthodoxy" to be objectionable. These objections are consistent with Calvin's conviction that no one is good enough or wise enough to define orthodoxy for all time, even though Calvin himself was sometimes famously unwilling to tolerate dissent.

The Church as Evangelical and Reformed

It is common to refer to Calvin, Luther, and the other Reformers as "evangelical." This is because the word "evangelical" comes from the Greek word *euangelion*, which means "gospel" or "good news." Reformers such as Luther and Calvin were attempting to recover the basic truths—the good news of the gospel. As we now know, being evangelical in the sixteenth century meant preaching the gospel of justification by grace through faith. According to Calvin and Luther, it was "*the* article upon which the church stands or falls."

Yet to be saved by God's grace means that the church is called to an ongoing reexamination of itself in the light of the Word of God. This self-assessment is at the heart of what it means to be "reformed." The word "re-form" means literally to fashion, shape, or render something anew. To re-form the church, then, is not merely to retrieve a set of beliefs from the past. It is a mistake to identify "the Reformed tradition" with an unchanging set of beliefs. That would be the very opposite of a tradition that aims always to reform itself. For Calvin the reform of the church meant that not only doctrine, but worship, practices, and indeed, the whole of life were to be subject always to the living and dynamic Word of God. He also believed that reform is the task of the whole church, and not just one wing of the church that adopts the name "Reformed."

Reformed Confessional Identity

Given the very nature of what it means to be "reformed," the definition of what qualifies as a "Reformed church" has never been clear. Since reform is an ongoing enterprise, there has never been a single authority within the Reformed family of churches empowered to determine which churches are genuinely Reformed and which are not. Reformed churches do not recognize a single human head of the church, as in Roman Catholicism. Nor have all the Reformed churches accepted a single authoritative confession, as the Lutherans did with the Augsburg Confession. Likewise no single creed has been vested with the power to state the boundaries of Reformed identity once and for all. Instead, the Reformed family of churches has allowed a plurality of confessions and creeds. This plurality was based on the conviction that confessions and creeds are always contextual, focusing on a particular set of issues and facts at a particular time. Reformed churches remain open, in principle, to new ways of understanding the faith in light of Scripture, as is clear from new confessions, such as Barmen and the Confession of 1967, that have arisen over the years.

Another reason for this plurality of confessions was the conviction that creeds and councils can err. No human being, nor any human assembly, is infallible. As proof of this, Calvin pointed to the council in the New Testament that decided to condemn and crucify Christ. Today we recognize that even a creed as respected as the Apostles' Creed is not perfect. For instance, it moves directly from its first affirmation about God and creation to a second about Jesus Christ. In so doing, the Apostles' Creed completely skips over the history of God's covenant with Israel, which is crucial if one wishes to understand Jesus' role as prophet, priest, and king. Furthermore, when the creed turns to Jesus, missing is any mention of his preaching, teaching, or healing ministries.

Given that the confessions and creeds of the Reformed churches are many and varied, and given that they are human creations that are not infallible, might there be still newer confessions or creeds adopted in the future? The answer is that historically there is an open-endedness to Reformed confessionalism. At any point, new confessions of faith are permissible, since being "reformed" does not signify a final state of perfection but an ongoing task. For that reason, Calvin's heirs in the Netherlands adopted the motto "the church reformed and always being reformed in accordance with the Word of God" (*ecclesia reformata, semper reformanda, secundum verbum Dei*).

Church Leadership

The doctrine of the priesthood of all believers implied the spiritual equality of all Christians before God. This meant that the leadership of the church was shared by the whole community. No single person or office was given power to carry out discipline or exercise the rights of church governance.

Church Offices

What should the leadership of the church look like? Based on his reading of the New Testament, Calvin divided church leaders into four offices: pastors, elders, deacons, and doctors (or teachers).[2] One of Calvin's main contributions was to develop a rationale for this variety of ministries. Calvin maintained that each office provided for a division of labor, not a differentiation of status. That is, all believers in the church are considered to be equal in the eyes of God. Calvin did not even use the term "laity," for he did not want to hint at any difference in rank between pastors and the rest of the church membership.

The office of *pastor* was charged with the primary responsibility for preaching and administration of the sacraments. From a practical point of view the role of preaching was central. How could it be otherwise for a church that places so much emphasis upon knowing, explaining, and proclaiming the Word of God in Scripture? To be sure, the Scriptures could be studied and explained by anyone. But the importance of pastors who are trained in the biblical languages cannot be emphasized enough. In an ultimate sense, Reformed churches entrusted their future to God. In a practical and penultimate sense, the vitality of Reformed churches has always depended on the power of learned preaching.

While Calvin believed that pastors were the ones who should administer the sacraments, he was clear that the clergy were not priests whose actions repeated the sacrifice of Christ, as the Roman Catholic Church taught. To the contrary, Christ's own sacrifice was a once-and-for-all event that was both effective and sufficient for our salvation.

In keeping with the priesthood of all believers, Calvin advocated a collegial understanding of the pastoral ministry. According to Calvin, distinctions such as cardinal, archbishop, bishop, and the like had no place in the ministry of Jesus Christ.

The office of *doctor* or *teacher* fulfilled a role similar to that of the pastor. Like pastors, teachers were charged with the task of interpreting Scripture. But they did not preach or administer the sacraments. Theirs was principally an educational role, often focused on teaching the young. Today the closest analogue is a seminary or divinity school professor.

Elders had responsibility for spiritual oversight of the congregation together with the pastors. In Geneva elders served along with pastors on the consistory, which meant they had responsibility for the spiritual well-being of the congregation, including discipline and the correction of morals.

The office of *deacon* was very important in Calvin's understanding of the church. Deacons had responsibility for the care of the poor, the sick, the needy, and the disabled. They were also responsible for the collection and distribution of monetary gifts for the poor and needy. Calvin based this form of ministry on passages such as Acts 6:1–6, where Stephen and others were appointed and ordained, with the laying on of hands, to carry out a ministry of compassion. Based on his reading of Scripture, Calvin also set up a separate order of women who served the same roles, but who were not ordained.

Calvin was insistent that church leaders were set aside "by no human choice but by the command of God and Christ alone" (*Inst.* 4.3.13, 2:1064). Ministers had to be elected by a vote of the people. Those ordained were ordinarily set apart through prayer and the laying on of hands. Ironically, however, we have no record of Calvin himself being officially ordained. Calvin lamented that the choice of church leaders had fallen on such bad times in the sixteenth century. There was little focus on call and no meaningful theological examination of candidates. Calvin complained that even ten-year-old boys were made bishops in order to shore up family power.

Leadership and the Marks of the Church

As you can imagine, there was much debate in Calvin's day over how to distinguish a true from a false church. Calvin answered this through his teaching on the "marks of the church." The church exists, said Calvin, where these two marks exist: (a) the Word is rightly preached, and (b) the sacraments are rightly administered.

Some of the Reformed confessions also added a so-called third mark, the administration of discipline. Calvin certainly was an advocate of discipline in the church. The main instrument of discipline in the Genevan church was the consistory, a committee made up of ministers and elders, presided over by a city magistrate. The consistory dealt primarily with matters of behavior, including non-Reformed religious practices, financial disputes, marital strife, issues of sexual fidelity, and personal conflicts of various sorts. The level of social control mandated by the consistory was far beyond what would be acceptable in a modern society. The mere accusation of engaging in some offensive practice could land a person before the consistory for judgment.

Yet there was a spiritual purpose behind church discipline. One purpose was to prevent people from falsely claiming to be Christian. Another was to protect the elect from the corrupting behavior of unrepentant and sinning reprobates. In all cases, the hope was that discipline would cause genuine repentance and lead to a person's restoration. Often the consistory acted with moderation and gentleness and performed a role that today would qualify as pastoral counseling. In a society that used to be dominated by individual confession before a Roman Catholic priest, the consistory practiced a more communal exercise of discernment, correction, and wisdom. Even when the consistory imposed an order of excommunication, prohibiting a person from receiving the Lord's Supper, such an action was not permanent. The person could be readmitted to the sacrament upon repentance.

Leadership: Avoiding Schism

Calvin considered it a grave matter to separate from the church, so long as the Word was being rightly preached and the sacraments administered. He rebuked anyone who arrogantly left a Christian body.

But how does one know the Word is being rightly preached? Given Calvin's teaching on Christian freedom, we would expect the focus of "right preaching" to be on major issues and Christian beliefs and not "things indifferent."

Accordingly, Calvin distinguished essential from nonessential doctrines. The list of essentials was short. It included belief that "God is one; Christ is God and the Son of God; our salvation rests in God's mercy; and the like" (*Inst.* 4.1.12, 2:1026). Calvin declared that there are many doctrines over which reasonable Christians may differ. Disagreement over nonessential matters is not sufficient to justify a schism. Calvin urged believers to listen to one another, quoting 1 Corinthians 14:30: "If a revelation is made to someone else sitting nearby, let the first person be silent." He also noted that in Corinth the entire congregation was infected with error, yet Paul recommends no schism. Instead the apostle calls the Corinthians to claim and live out their unity in Christ.

As we know, Calvin considered the Roman Catholic Church to be gravely in error, but this did not mean it had altogether ceased to be a church of Jesus Christ. Its hierarchy was corrupt. But Calvin believed that a true church might still exist in parts of the Roman Church wherever priests were rightly preaching the Word and rightly administering the sacraments.

The Church's Mission

Under Calvin's leadership, Geneva became an engine of mission. Calvin held that the gospel should be preached to all peoples, no matter what their social class—the king as well as the humblest peasant (Commentary on 1 Tim. 2:4). Partly through the vagaries of history and partly by design, Geneva had become a city of refugees from all over Europe. As circumstances permitted these refugees returned home and carried Calvin's version of the gospel with them. Around 1555 the pastors in Geneva began commissioning missionaries to various parts of Europe, but especially to Calvin's native France.

Almost all of Calvin's activity was concentrated in Europe. This was in part because the reform movement was fighting for its very survival. Under these conditions, it is a wonder they could manage to support any missionaries at all. Still, in 1556 Calvin supported a Huguenot missionary endeavor to Brazil, though it ended in failure. By comparison, Roman Catholics sent missionaries all over the world. But we must remember that this was in part because, with few exceptions, sixteenth-century missionary activity was identical with empire expansion and colonization. The Huguenot mission was itself part of an effort to establish a foreign colony in Brazil.

Always Reforming:
The Church in a Post-Christendom Age

Calvin's ideas about the church, powerful though they are, presuppose the existence of a coherent Christian civilization, or what is known as "Christendom." In Christendom everything in the broader culture works to support the existence of the church. This means that the rulers of the world are supposed to protect and defend the cause of Christ. In turn, the church provides the moral values for the society.

Today, however, this coherent Christian civilization is no more. In the United States and elsewhere, church and state have been separated by law. This is good, for having a nationally sponsored church suppresses the rights of those citizens who believe differently. The fate of Servetus is but an extreme example of this. Since their heyday in the 1950s, the Protestant churches in America have gradually lost their prominence in terms of moral, social, and cultural influence. There was a time when stores were closed and no one would dare to schedule a ball game on a Sunday morning. That too has changed. To be sure, vestiges of Christendom remain. People continue to nurture a vague belief in God; churches and their ministers are still given tax breaks under the law. But by and large, Western Christians face the challenge of how to organize the church in a post-Christendom situation.

Some dimensions of Calvin's thought can help us. Calvin's conviction that the church is more than its structures or bureaucracy is still true. The church is even more than its doctrines or traditions. Calvin was clear that our allegiance should not be to a particular branch of the Christian tradition but to the gospel. And the gospel, as Paul summed it up, is "the power of God for salvation" (Rom. 1:16). Calvin would have been as alarmed that well-meaning Christians defend something called "Calvinism" or "Presbyterianism" or "Congregationalism" as he was that powerful men in his own day defended something called "Roman Catholicism." The thought that the gospel could be reduced to any sort of "ism" would have struck him as a grave error.

In response to his strong convictions about what the gospel demanded, Calvin did something new, something very risky. Christians today may be called to do the same. The ways of conceiving and organizing the church that worked in a Christendom age are not likely to work today. Imitating Calvin is not the answer; it will not move us forward. Recapturing Calvin's reforming spirit, however, may be a good start.

A pervasive worry some people feel today is that Western churches are losing members and consequently losing power. Calvin would have found this concern exceedingly strange. In contrast to Calvin's day, when Protestant churches were threatened by foreign armies and dissident Christians lived in survival mode, today Western Christians live in relative security and still control an unprecedented amount of wealth and influence. The crisis of the mainline churches, Calvin might counsel us, is not a crisis of power but of meaning. Both the people who still inhabit the pews, as well as those who have long since left the pews, are asking real questions about the meaning of religious faith. What they need is ongoing, biblically grounded dialogue in which the challenges and issues of the contemporary world are placed in direct conversation with the Bible. One of Calvin's strongest gifts was his ability to make a cogent case for the Christian faith that was persuasive not only to his generation but to many generations after. What we need today is a new way to speak about the Christian faith that takes seriously the questions and doubts that people have without simply denying them.

At the end of the day, I also suspect that Calvin would see the challenge ahead as primarily a crisis not of circumstances but of leadership. Calvin spent much of his time pouring his life into shaping a generation of people who were equipped to *be* the church. Like the young man who marched into Noyon and renounced his income from a corrupt church, we too may need to find the courage to let go of the past and the willingness to lead and be led into new ways of being church—and of serving the God who is still our hope for years to come.

Questions for Discussion

1. How do you experience the church—as a human institution or a divine creation? Why? Is there a third position?
2. What criteria do most people use in order to decide what congregation to join? How important is theology in this decision?
3. Name some reasons why there is no single creed or confession that defines what it means to be Reformed.
4. How does your congregation view church discipline? What sorts of behaviors might warrant church discipline? How does church discipline differ from pastoral care or counseling?

5. How might Calvin's insights about disagreements and church schism inform our present atmosphere of ecclesial disagreement and unrest?

6. What kinds of activities and pressures compete with church life in your community? Name some ways that Christians in your community can meet these challenges.

Chapter 10

Connecting to God

Worship and Sacraments

*M*edieval Catholicism was marked by a vast range of devotional practices. Embarking on pilgrimages, venerating relics, invoking the intercession of Mary and the saints, engaging in regular confession and acts
of penance, and participating in the rhythms of the Christian calendar—
in all these ways, ordinary Christians hoped to gain spiritual merit. As
a young boy Calvin himself had been immersed in this merit-based spir
ituality. For example, Calvin was made by his mother to pay homage to
various relics of the saints. As an adult he would reject all this, writing
with especially biting sarcasm about the practice of venerating relics.
He wryly noted that cathedrals spread around Europe had enough supposed splinters of the cross of Christ to launch a fleet of ships.

Many of these devotional practices were called into question by
the Protestant theology of justification by grace through faith. If salvation occurs not through a person's good works but by relying on
the mercy of God alone, then the merit-seeking activity of medieval
Christians was pointless. However, Protestants did not purge devotional practices from the Christian life completely; instead, they
developed their own practices, informed by their own theology, in
order to support their own view of salvation and the Christian life.

Worship and the Spiritual Life

Preaching

Calvin developed a unique approach to worship and the spiritual life.
First and foremost, he placed a strong premium on the power and

intelligibility of preaching.[1] This meant that hearing the Bible explained and taught in sermons became all-important. A true church exists, said Calvin, where the Word of God is rightly preached and the sacraments rightly administered. The danger in this definition, of course, was that, over time, the passive virtue of "hearing" would become more important than the active virtue of "doing." Calvin's answer, no doubt, would be that God's people must first hear rightly in order to know how to do rightly. Also, in Calvin's own context, the role of the consistory was to assure that hearing and doing were both kept in focus.

This religious emphasis on knowing the Word of God in Scripture dovetailed with the rise of adult literacy in the general population. People who could now read the Scriptures were eager to hear them explained in a Sunday sermon. It also coincided with a rising middle class in the cities, providing Protestant preachers with a growing audience for a message that was fresh and liberating. These new Protestant laypeople developed a curiosity about the intellectual dimensions of the faith, and preachers like Calvin were only too happy to oblige them. The net effect was to narrow the gap between those who were educated and those who were not. Over time, the study of the Bible became a central feature of Reformed piety.

Much of Calvin's own life was taken up with communicating the Word. Some weeks he preached every day. He also lectured on the Bible and Christian theology multiple times a week. His approach to Scripture was to offer line-by-line commentary. Calvin's remarks were faithfully recorded by scribes and have come down to us in an impressive collection of biblical commentaries and sermons. One thousand five hundred of Calvin's sermons have survived to this day, but another eight hundred were thoughtlessly destroyed in the nineteenth century by inept librarians.

Calvin believed that when a preacher preached faithfully, it was as though God were speaking directly to the congregation. One of the main convictions of the Reformation in Zurich, Geneva, and elsewhere in the Swiss regions was that "the preaching of the Word of God *is* the Word of God" (Second Helvetic Confession).

Christian Education and Confirmation

Given Calvin's emphasis on knowing and understanding the Word of God, it is not surprising that he promoted what we today call Christian education. One of the first things Calvin did during his first tenure in Geneva was to write a catechism (1537). When he was called back to Geneva in 1541 he wrote an improved catechism that appeared in French (1542) and in Latin (1545). The goal of Calvin's catechism was to make sure the young Christian knew the basics of the Apostles' Creed, the Ten Commandments, and the Lord's Prayer.

When it came to church membership, Calvin declared that confirmation was *not* an official sacrament of the church, in contrast to Roman Catholic practice. Instead confirmation was a formal instruction in the faith leading to a profession of faith and church membership.

Emphasis on Simplicity

In contrast to the extravagance of medieval devotional practices, the accent in Reformed spirituality was upon simplicity. Calvin considered much of the spirituality of the medieval church to be at best a massive distraction, and at worst an exercise in pagan superstition.

Especially offensive to Calvin was the abundance of images depicting the Divine. Based on the prohibition of graven images in the Ten Commandments, Calvin urged the orderly removal of such images from Protestant houses of worship. Calvin did not oppose all images, only those that depicted Deity. Prior to Calvin's arrival in Geneva, the city had witnessed a riotous destruction of images (1535).

All Time Is God's Time

In addition, the Reformed faith de-emphasized the church calendar. There was no special observance of Christmas in Geneva, and Calvin eliminated the rituals associated with Lent, the forty-day period from Ash Wednesday until Easter Saturday symbolic of Jesus' time of temptation in the wilderness (Matt. 4:1–3; Luke 4:1–3). In the medieval church a Lenten fast was required, consisting of abstaining from meat and dairy products. Refusing to keep the Lenten fast had became one of the hallmarks of Reformed Protestantism ever since a group of citizens gathered to eat sausages in Zurich on Ash Wednesday in 1522. Calvin did not oppose fasting for special purposes, but he maintained that the whole of life should be a fast.

Despite the relative austerity of Calvin' piety, it would be incorrect to conclude that the Reformed faith was completely devoid of passion or feeling. One strong feature of Reformed worship was the metrical singing of the Psalms. Calvin himself was largely responsible for encouraging this practice, which he had first encountered in German-speaking Strassburg. After creating a French version of the Psalter in Strassburg, Calvin carried the practice of singing the Psalms with him to Geneva. Several versions appeared over the years, culminating in a complete Geneva Psalter that was published in 1551 under the editorial direction of Calvin's young lieutenant, Theodore Beza. The practice of Psalms singing then made its way into France, through Calvinist missionaries, and was formational for Huguenot piety. The robust singing of the Psalms saw the Huguenots through many a year of bitter persecution.

Expanded Spiritual Roles for the Laity

Another distinctive dimension of Reformed faith and practice was the empowerment of the laity. The offices of elder and deacon gave ordinary laypeople important spiritual and social responsibilities that had previously been the exclusive domain of the clergy. Under Calvin's guidance, the Genevan consistory, the body responsible for exercising spiritual oversight of the city, included both clergy and laity. In addition, oversight of almsgiving and care for the poor were now the responsibilities of the deacons. As noted earlier, Reformed piety sought to minimize the distinction between clergy and laity. The only difference between the two, at least in theory, was one of spiritual gifts and pastoral responsibilities rather than of status. To symbolize this new sharing of spiritual power, Reformed pastors ceased wearing elaborate church vestments. Instead, ministers who presided at the Lord's Supper wore a simple black Geneva gown, attire that would have been considered ordinary street clothes. Ironically, today the Geneva gown, the standard garb of a scholar in Calvin's time, has once again become a vestment that distinguishes clergy from laity.

Sacraments

The word "sacrament" never appears in the New Testament. It derives from a classical Latin word, *sacramentum*, which referred to a soldier's oath of allegiance sealed by a tattoo, or by the smearing of blood on the soldier's chest. Because of its origins, the very idea of a sacrament could be seen as pagan. Nevertheless, the word "sacrament" was used in the medieval period to translate the Greek New Testament word *mysterion*, literally, "mystery."

Augustine defined a sacrament as an outward and visible sign of an inward and spiritual grace. This definition is illuminating but also open-ended. Many things could fit this definition: a handshake, a kiss, the ordinary sharing of a meal—each of these can be an outward sign of something inward and spiritual. One can even say that there is a sacramental quality to the universe as a whole, inasmuch as nature can be said to reflect the glory of God.

Nevertheless, for Calvin, and for Protestants in general, the sacraments needed to be firmly connected to God's concrete promise of salvation in Jesus Christ.[2] According to Calvin, the sacraments are an "appendix" to the Word. That is, they function much like sermon illustrations. Sacraments are living illustrations of God's grace, enacted glimpses of God's love and rule. But because Calvin viewed the preaching of the Word as central to faith and the sacraments as secondary, he could not imagine allowing a sacrament without a sermon. For Calvin, no preaching of the Word meant no sacrament.

All this led Calvin to a view completely different from Roman Catholicism about the number of sacraments and how they work. The medieval Roman Catholic Church had seven sacraments. Calvin reduced the number of sacraments to two, baptism and the Lord's Supper, because only these two had specifically been commanded by Christ. (This ignores footwashing, which was commanded by Christ too.) Baptism is the once-only sacrament that marks our initiation into the covenant of grace and the community of faith. The Lord's Supper (or Eucharist) is the repeated sacrament that sustains us as believers, in which we can experience an authentic encounter with the risen Christ as we partake of the bread and cup in his name.

In addition to baptism and Eucharist, the sacraments of the medieval church included penance, confirmation, marriage, ordination, and anointing the sick. The way all seven of these sacraments were conceived in Roman Catholicism hinged on a particular understanding of the church and a related understanding of ministry. The church was conceived by Rome as a hierarchical institution upon which the laity must depend for their spiritual health. Similarly, Rome conceived of ministry as the priestly dispensation of grace. Indeed, the sacraments are effective to convey grace merely by being rightly administered by the priest. In this way everything depended upon the power of the clerical class.

Calvin's understanding of the sacraments operated with a different view of the church and its ministry. First, the church is a community of the chosen, not a hierarchical institution—hence the shift from the medieval "Mass" to the Protestant "Lord's Supper." Consequently, this more communal focus required the translation of the worship service into the common language of the people and the distribution of both the bread and the cup to the laity. Second, this changed view of the sacraments was part of a changed view of ministry. In the Catholic Mass, the very performance of the act by the priest conveys grace automatically. By contrast, Calvin followed Luther in believing that each communicant must exercise faith in order to receive the benefit of the sacrament. The sacraments for Calvin do not *dispense* grace so much as they *proclaim* grace. That is, by the power of the Holy Spirit, in the presence of faith, the sacraments become an occasion in which the grace of God is made real.

Baptism

Baptism with water is the sign of a Christian's initiation into the community of faith. The washing with water symbolizes our cleansing from sin by the work of Christ. It is a visible enactment of our commitment to put to death our old sinful ways in order to live in union with Christ, in ways that are pleasing to God.

But if baptism is a sign of our dying and rising with Christ, then how can it be appropriate to baptize infants, who are not yet able to own the spiritual life for themselves? Calvin's answer was to think in terms of God's covenant with Israel. God's covenant was with the whole people of God, including children. We know this because God commanded the circumcision of eight-day-old boys as a sign of their inclusion in the Abrahamic covenant. Similarly in the book of Acts, when Peter instructs people to repent and be baptized, he adds that "the promise is for you, *for your children*, and for all who are far away, everyone whom the Lord our God calls to him" (Acts 2:39). Thus according to Peter the promises of Christ extend to the children of believers. Just as circumcision was the sign of God's inclusion of children in the covenant made with Abraham, so infant baptism is the sign confirming God's inclusion of children in the new covenant made in Christ.

Other questions regarding infant baptism remain. Earlier I said that there is no authentic sacrament without the presence of faith. Then how can we baptize an infant, in whom faith is not yet evident? Calvin's answer is that faith *is*, in fact, evident through believing parents who, with the support of their congregation, promise to raise the child "in the nurture and admonition of the Lord." Passing on the faith to the next generations is serious business, and in the Reformed tradition the spiritual nurture of children has always been the shared responsibility of the parents (or guardians) and the whole community of faith. This is where confirmation gets its name. When a child is confirmed, (s)he takes as his/her own the faith of the community—in essence saying yes to what the community has already done to make the gospel real in his or her life.

One further question has been at the center of controversy about baptism: is it necessary for salvation? Calvin disagreed with the Roman Catholic view that baptism is necessary for salvation. In keeping with his high view of divine sovereignty, Calvin insisted that God is free to save whomever God wills. In other words, God's power to save cannot be limited by or enabled by the sacramental actions of human priests or ministers. Hence God is most surely able to save a person who has never been baptized. Because baptism is not necessary for salvation, Calvin also rejected the need for nurses or other laypeople to administer so-called emergency baptisms.

Lord's Supper

The biblical origins of this meal remain something of a puzzle. Was the meal that Jesus commanded his disciples to continue "in remembrance of him" a ritual daily meal conducted in a spirit of fellowship (agape meal)? Or was it tied more particularly to Jesus' sacrificial death on the cross (a solemn memorial meal)? Or was it more of a prophetic meal in anticipation of the messianic banquet at the end of days (a celebration of God's coming heavenly reign)? Perhaps it was all these things.

Elements of each have entered into Christian reflection on the significance of the Lord's Supper. Calvin notes that this sacrament is both a gift of grace *from God to us*—hence it is the *"Lord's* Supper"— as well as an occasion for giving of thanks *from us to God*—thus it is also the *"Eucharist"* (from the Greek word for thanksgiving).

Yet despite all the various meanings attached to it, the Lord's Supper for Calvin and his Protestant colleagues was emphatically *not* a ritual resacrifice of Christ, as it was for the Roman Catholic Church. In the Catholic Mass the priest reenacts the sacrifice of Christ at the altar. By contrast, Protestant theology considered the sacrifice of Christ to be unique, Christ's death as offered "once for all" (Heb. 10:10). No human act, priestly or otherwise, is able to repeat this uniqueness. The Eucharist was the pure gift of God's promise to us. Consequently, Protestants replaced the Roman Catholic altar, with its connotations of sacrifice, with the simple Communion table, representing the rustic dinner table around which Jesus and his disciples gathered. Protestants also rejected the Roman Catholic doctrine of transubstantiation, according to which the elements remain bread and wine only in appearance but are transformed into the actual body and blood of Jesus Christ by the words of institution spoken by the priest during the Mass.

Although Protestants agreed with one another in their rejection of the Roman Catholic Mass, they differed among themselves over how to think about the positive meaning of the Lord's Supper. Much of the debate centered on precisely what transpires during the sacred meal. Calvin spent much of his ministry trying to propose a mediating solution that would resolve the disagreement.

Calvin argued that the Supper provides real spiritual nourishment in which believers receive the benefits of the broken body and shed blood of Christ. But, at the same time, it is not an event in which something magical happens to the bread and wine. The body and blood of Christ are not "locally present" in the bread and wine. Instead, it is the presence of the Holy Spirit in the Supper that enables believers to truly participate with Christ. Yet this participation does bring about a true partaking of the spiritual substance of Christ's body and blood.

Calvin's mediating position is best understood when seen in comparison to the positions of Martin Luther in Germany and of Calvin's fellow Reformed theologians in Zurich, Huldrych Zwingli (1483– 1531) and Heinrich Bullinger (1504–1575).

First, Calvin agreed with Luther that there is a "real presence" of Christ in the Supper. In denying the "local presence" of Christ's body and blood in the meal, however, Calvin disagreed with Luther's contention that Christ's body and blood are "in, with, and under" the elements. This was possible, in Luther's view, because after the resurrection Christ's body was "ubiquitous"—it was everywhere. But it was especially present in the Eucharist, whereby the faith of believers is sustained, and unbelievers drink judgment upon themselves (cf. 1 Cor. 11:27). Calvin rejected this part of Luther's view, however, arguing that the body of Christ could not be everywhere, because Jesus Christ had already ascended into heaven. When asked where was the body of Christ, Calvin's answer was straightforward: Jesus' body is "seated at the right hand of God the Father Almighty," as the Apostles' Creed asserts.

Second, Calvin agreed with Zwingli that Christ's presence is a "spiritual presence" in the hearts of believers. However, Calvin also thought the Lord's Supper is a "means of grace." That is, the meal itself is instrumental in bringing about a spiritual transformation for believers who partake. By contrast, Zwingli understood the Lord's Supper to be a communal celebration, not a meal that dispenses grace. Zwingli drew a strong distinction between the sacramental "sign" (bread and wine) and the thing it "signified" (the body and blood of Christ). Zwingli believed, furthermore, that the words, "This is my body, broken for you" (1 Cor. 11:24), mean "this *signifies* my body. . . ." Thus for Zwingli the Lord's Supper was a memorial meal in which believers, in a communal act, remember the death and resurrection of Christ. There is a real presence of Christ in the meal, but it is a spiritual presence located in the internal partaking of the elements by believers in faith.

Calvin agreed with Zwingli and the Zurich theology that "this is my body" should not be taken literally. He also agreed that there is a distinction between the sign and the thing signified. But Calvin always insisted that we not understand the *distinction* between bread and wine (the sign) and body and blood (the thing signified) as a *disjunction*. This led Calvin to reject what he perceived as Zwingli's reducing the Lord's Supper to a "mere memorial." In Zwingli's last published work (which Calvin had probably not read) it is clear that Zwingli considered the Lord's Supper to be more than a "mere memorial." Be that as it may, Calvin was adamant that believers do more than remember Christ in the meal. For Calvin the bread and wine truly "exhibit" the body and blood of Christ.

It is ironic and tragic that a sacred meal designed to unite Christian believers as one body has become the cause of so much division. To his credit, Calvin worked tirelessly to end the division. Although he was never able to reach an agreement with the Lutherans, one of Calvin's greatest successes was an agreement he worked out with Zwingli's successor in Zurich, Heinrich Bullinger.

Despite their differences Calvin and Bullinger arrived at a compromise statement on the Lord's Supper in 1549 that both Geneva and Zurich accepted.[3] The agreement was called the "Zurich Consent," or in Latin, the *Consensus Tigurinus*. In 1551 the statement was accepted by the major Swiss cities. This agreement is important historically, because it is only with the Zurich Consent that one can begin to speak meaningfully of a common "Reformed theology."

The consent was successful because Calvin and Bullinger were able to honor the deeply held convictions of the other. They agreed that the point of worship and the sacraments is to lead believers to Christ. They agreed that the gospel is primary and the sacraments are a secondary "appendix" or "seal" to help bring the promise of the gospel alive in the hearts and minds of the faithful. They honored Calvin's concern that the sacraments facilitate union with Christ. They also honored the emphasis in Zurich on the meal as the public seal of a communal celebration in which the faith of the community is expressed and deepened. They agreed that something happens in the meal as a gracious gesture from God to us (Calvin) and a response of gratitude from us to God (Zurich). But they were careful to deny that the sacrament, in itself, carries with it salvation. We are made partakers of Christ, but only by the power of the Holy Spirit. Grace is offered to all, but grace is effective only for those who receive the sacrament in faith. There is an "eating of the flesh of Christ" but it happens only "figuratively."

Always Reforming: The Sacraments as a Call to Unity

Calvin's theology reflects a fundamental reform of baptism and the Lord's Supper, yet even more reform may be needed in our own day.

Calvinist churches allow for baptism of infants on the grounds that God's promises belong not only to adults but to their children. But our practice of baptizing infants can inadvertently become a celebration of Christianity as a cultural heritage, rather than a serious commitment to the Christian formation of our children. How often have you heard parents refer to the baptism of their baby as "getting the child *done*"? How often has a baptism become the excuse for extravagant baptismal gowns and lavish after-church parties? These lapses do not, of themselves, invalidate infant baptism. It is still right to believe that the covenant extends to our children. But revitalizing the theology of infant baptism in a highly pluralistic culture remains a challenge.

Regarding the Lord's Supper, much was changed by Calvin and his peers, including their rejection of the idea that Christ's sacrifice is repeated in the Roman Catholic Mass each time Communion is given. Yet Calvin and his colleagues did not do enough to prevent the Lord's Supper from becoming a point of division. Nor has the tradition done enough to assure that the meal is understood as a joyous celebration of the anticipated messianic banquet in which people are joined from north, south, east, and west to share fellowship with one another and with God.

Perhaps the framework hammered out by Calvin and Bullinger still offers us the best way forward. It shows us that forever squabbling over the mode of Christ's presence is neither necessary nor edifying. In addition, it demonstrates that Reformed theology can tolerate a range of opinions even on so central a subject as the sacraments. If mutual forbearance is possible on an issue this pivotal, then it ought to be possible on other issues as well. By working to build consensus, even when full agreement was impossible, Calvin and Bullinger not only honored one another's consciences but modeled the very unity to which the sacraments themselves call us.

Questions for Discussion

1. Name some Protestant devotional practices. How do they enable Christians to grow in their faith? Why did Calvin refer to many of the devotional practices of his day as "superstition"?

2. What place does the Bible have in the preaching that you hear most often? What place does the Bible have in contemporary worship services that you have attended? How important is Bible study in the life of your congregation?

3. The Second Helvetic Confession says that "the preaching of the Word of God *is* the Word of God." What does this mean? Describe a time when you felt that God was speaking to you through a sermon.

4. What do you make of Calvin's refusal to observe Christmas and Lent? Why do you think he was against these observances? What would Calvin think of contemporary Christian music? What would he think of pastors who wear street clothes in the pulpit?

5. How are preaching and the sacraments linked in your congregation? How is the Word of God proclaimed in home, shut-in, or hospital Communion services? How is it proclaimed when there is a baptism? What would Calvin think of private baptisms done apart from a regular worship service?

6. Why are Christians today not very concerned about the specifics of how Christ is present in the Lord's Supper? Why was this such a burning issue in Calvin's day? Describe a time when you felt the presence of Christ in the sacrament of Communion.

Chapter 11

Politics, Economy, and Society

Worldly thought and action were very important to Calvin—so important that he concluded both the *Institutes* (written for the educated) and his first catechism (written for children) with a chapter on the power and role of civil government. This was a bit unusual. Ordinarily, we might expect a work in Christian theology to conclude with the resurrection and eternal life. Calvin certainly believed in these things and wrote about them. But he chose to bring his major theological work to a climax with reflections *not* on the world to come but on our political responsibility for *this* world.

Why was Calvin so concerned with politics? One obvious answer is that Calvin and his associates had been the victims of government-sponsored persecution. One of Calvin's aims, then, was defensive: to convince rulers that Christian reformers did not intend political revolt. But there was also a more constructive reason. Calvin's brand of reform sought to bring all of life under the lordship of Christ. Among other things, this meant that both rulers and their subjects were accountable to God. Religious beliefs have public consequences. Religious reform was meant to lead to social, political, and economic reform. And all of this was to be pursued for the glory of God.

Politics

Calvin's success in Geneva was due in significant part to his perceptive attention to politics.[1] He had a gift for organization and a knack for reading political situations. He also had a keen interest in the activity of politicians and government leaders. In the *Institutes* he discussed which form of government was the best—monarchy, aristocracy, or democracy. Although he thought that each system had its pros and cons, he was a critic of the absolute power of kings. He invoked countless biblical examples of Israel's failed kings, and wrote specifically about the problems with the monarchical form of government. Though he was respectful when writing to monarchs (such as Francis I or Queen Elizabeth of England), he also could level the charge in his public lectures that "if one could uncover the hearts of kings, he would find hardly one in a hundred who does not despise everything divine." In the end, Calvin favored a blend of aristocracy and democracy.

Calvin's positive evaluation of the role of government contrasts with Luther, for example, who talked about politics as a dirty business, in which God is at work only in a backhanded way. For Luther politics was a "necessary evil." On the other hand, for the non-Reformed Anabaptists politics was an "unnecessary evil," which good Christians should avoid. Over against these views, Calvin believed one could do good in the political arena so long as the political institutions that were ordained by God were made accountable to God. Therefore, Calvin had no hesitation in preaching truth to power, calling political leaders to consider their actions in the light of the Word of God.

Almost every year of Calvin's ministry, the crackdown of Roman Catholic powers against Protestant minorities intensified. These persecutions in Germany, England, Scotland, and especially in France caused Calvin to refine some of his political views. Prior to the increase in persecutions, Calvin believed what most people of his age believed: that passive obedience to political authority is a Christian duty. Calvin based this on Romans 13:1–7, a passage in which Paul admonished Christians to submit themselves to worldly rulers. From this Calvin argued that people should show honor to the office, even if the person holding the office was a scoundrel or worse. God had providentially willed these rulers to rule, Calvin reasoned, and this meant that to submit to them was to submit to the will of God.

Yet with the worsening violence, Calvin began to change his mind and to flirt with the possibility of active resistance against a godless ruler. The way Calvin worked this through was in keeping with his desire to root his arguments in Scripture. The breakthrough came with his reading of the biblical story of Daniel. Daniel was a Jew living in exile in the court of the Persian king Darius. Darius issued an order that all Jews in his court should be fed certain nonkosher rations. Daniel could not obey Darius's order without denying God. So what was he to do? Calvin found a clue in 1 Peter 2:17, "Fear God! Honor the emperor!" These two commandments are bound together; and yet Calvin maintained that the first must have priority, because kings derive their authority from God. If a king issues an edict that defies God, then that king ceases to be a true king and, in effect, sets himself outside the will of God and the rule of law. Consequently, the king's God-fearing subjects are free to disobey the offending command. In his commentary on Daniel 6:22, Calvin proclaimed: "earthly princes lay aside all their power when they rise up against God, and are unworthy of being reckoned in the number of mankind. We ought rather to defy than to obey them."

Calvin argued further that leaders who pursue ungodly policies relinquish their civil authority and (by implication) are subject to being disobeyed. In reaching this conclusion Calvin knew he had to walk a fine line. He knew he was putting forth a potentially revolutionary idea. So in order to reassure those in power, he was careful to deny that ordinary citizens acting on their own have a right to overthrow the king. Were Calvin to allow for such a right, he risked being written off as an advocate of mob rule, an anarchist.

Nevertheless, Calvin observed that in the Old Testament God raised up leaders to deliver the people from oppressive rulers. He went on to argue that duly appointed city officials (the magistrates) were empowered to protect the people from tyranny. Hence these officials should have the right to resist an ungodly king or prince.

Planting the Seeds of Democracy

Calvin wrote these comments about active resistance at a time when persecution was intensifying against his own people, the French Protestants, known as Huguenots. It was no accident that Calvin dedicated his Daniel commentary to these Protestants suffering persecution in France. In the decades ahead Calvin's native region of Picardy was to produce a disproportionate number of adherents to the reform movement, many of whom would die in the religious civil wars in

France (1562–1598) that began in Calvin's last years and raged long after his death.

The ensuing wars had a profound impact on how Calvin's political views were received by later generations. From the Reformed perspective, the most notorious event during these wars was the St. Bartholomew's Day Massacre, by far the worst massacre of the sixteenth century. Beginning on August 24, 1572, which was the Feast of St. Bartholomew, a wave of Catholic violence against the Huguenots broke out in Paris. Men, women, and children were butchered in the streets. The violence spread to other cities around France and lasted for months. The death toll numbered at least ten thousand, but some have estimated the number closer to one hundred thousand. Many prominent Huguenots were among the dead. Random outbreaks of violence happen in time of war, but this one was planned by French Catholic political leaders. Significantly, when news of the massacre reached Rome, the pope called for a celebration.

In the wake of the St. Bartholomew's Day Massacre, the survivors among the Huguenot leadership became more politically radical. Although Calvin was no longer alive to provide guidance, his brief comments about resistance against tyranny were pushed in a revolutionary direction by some of the Huguenot leaders. They argued that kings are given their power by the people and thus are answerable to the people, and that the hereditary rulership of the royal family was a mere custom and not written into the laws of nature. Rulers should be bound by constitutional principles.

Almost two hundred years later, in the years leading up to the events of 1776, similar arguments were made in the American colonies. This is not surprising, since some 70 percent of the population at the time of the revolution had been influenced by Calvinism. Revolutionary leaders such as the Calvinist minister John Witherspoon (the third president of Princeton University and a signer of the Declaration of Independence) looked to Calvin and the later Huguenot writers to buttress their belief in the power of the people and the right to oppose tyrannical government. They also drew to some extent upon Calvin's writings about the centrality of freedom.

The net effect was that Calvin's brief lines in the *Institutes* became one small link in the chain that led to modern democracy. Many of Calvin's followers would advocate constitutional theories of governmental power, resistance by the people (and not just by the magistrates) to tyranny, democratic forms of civil governance, and (eventually) principles of tolerance and human rights.

Some scholars have questioned whether the connection between Calvin and democracy was that strong. They observe that in the sixteenth century Calvin would have had trouble making sense of a fully democratic society that allowed freedom of religion and the separation of church and state. This is no doubt true. Many have gone further, however, claiming that Calvin's Geneva was a theocracy, a government ruled by clergy. Yet this was clearly not true. In Geneva religious and political power were distinguished. They ran on parallel but coordinated tracks, each with its own sphere of power. The civil government was supposed to uphold true worship, true doctrine, and upright behavior. The church was supposed to cultivate a righteous citizenry. In many ways this was a delicate dance in which neither side had absolute control.

As to whether Calvin contributed to the development of democracy, there is truth to both sides. Some of Calvin's actions seem repressive and even cruel and unjust by modern standards, the burning of Servetus being a prime example. At the same time, some of the principles Calvin espoused were humanitarian in nature and anticipated our modern concern for human rights.

Calvin's Greatest Sin: The Death of Michael Servetus

The execution of Michael Servetus (October 27, 1553) stood as the most notorious stain against Calvin's reputation. Servetus was a Spanish physician, an extremely intelligent man who studied the circulation of the blood and dabbled in theology. He may have been a descendant of Spanish Jews who had been forced to convert to Christianity. This might explain why his knowledge of Judaism far exceeded what the average sixteenth-century Christian would have known.

Servetus got into trouble on two major counts: he denied the doctrine of the Trinity and objected to infant baptism. In the sixteenth century this was enough to make Servetus a "hunted heretic" in a number of European cities, both Protestant and Catholic.[2] Servetus was targeted by the Catholic Inquisition, a tribunal charged with rooting out heresy. In April of 1553 Servetus narrowly escaped execution at Roman Catholic hands in the French city of Vienne. In August of that same year Servetus showed up in Geneva and was immediately arrested. Though he was a wanted man, he was discovered in the cathedral in Geneva calmly listening to Calvin preach.

After a dramatic trial, the city council voted to have him burned at the stake for blasphemy. Oddly enough, it may have been the denial of infant baptism that most aroused the opposition of the city council in Geneva. That would have put him in league with the Anabaptists, who were widely considered a threat to the city's political order.

Calvin is often blamed for what happened to Servetus. The two of them had carried on a heated correspondence over the years. Servetus once sent Calvin a copy of the *Institutes* annotated with Servetus's own strongly critical comments. One of Servetus's theological works was called *The Restitution of Christianity*. The word "restitution" may have been chosen in opposition to Calvin's word, "institution." Bitter remarks Calvin made about Servetus in various pieces of correspondence make clear that Calvin had little regard for the man. But was Calvin to blame for Servetus's death?

It is true that Calvin was one of the main witnesses for the prosecution against Servetus. He gave ample evidence of Servetus's doctrinal errors. But Servetus would not have been convicted if the city council had not believed him to be a threat. Those who claim that Calvin manipulated the city council to turn against Servetus forget that Servetus's arrest happened during a time when Calvin's enemies controlled the political reins of Geneva. Banking on this fact and knowing that he was a wanted man in many European cities, Servetus may have come to Geneva believing he could provoke a showdown with Calvin and win. In fact, the Geneva city council offered Servetus the choice of being tried in another city, but he preferred to take his chances with the Geneva authorities.

Calvin's defenders have long contended that, in opposing Servetus, Calvin was simply reflecting the beliefs of his age. This is true. Defenders also point out that Calvin pleaded with Servetus to give up his heretical beliefs. When Servetus was convicted, Calvin also urged the city council to carry out a more humane form of execution than burning Servetus alive. These factors do mitigate Calvin's guilt somewhat. But they do not absolve him of all responsibility.

Calvin, Tolerance, and Human Rights

From a modern perspective, the burning of Servetus is reprehensible. It is disappointing that Calvin, who knew so well what religious persecution felt like and who argued so eloquently that rulers should show forbearance to Protestants, was unable to demonstrate forbearance in the case of Servetus. Even worse, there is evidence that Calvin knew he could gain a political advantage through Servetus's demise. That Geneva dealt so decisively with such a notorious heretic solidified Calvin's international reputation as a force to be reckoned with.

It is also incorrect to assume that in the sixteenth century Calvin could not be expected to know any better. Some of Calvin's own contemporaries thought Servetus's execution to be cruel and unnecessary. One of Calvin's former students, Sebastian Castellio, strongly criticized Servetus's death sentence and wrote an impassioned plea arguing against the execution of heretics. Castellio argued that it is better to let a thousand heretics go free than to burn a single person who is innocent.

The reality is that Calvin's record is mixed. On the negative side, Calvin acquiesced in much of the brutality of his age. The city of Geneva engaged in the burning of women suspected of being witches. It succumbed to hysteria against people who were accused of spreading the plague. It routinely engaged in court-sponsored torture of defendants awaiting trial. When Calvin finally achieved the political majority he needed in 1555 to carry out his reform agenda, it was only after four of his fiercest opponents were executed. All of these points should give us serious pause.

On the positive side, Calvin often wrote passionately about human equality: "I say: we ought to embrace the whole human race without exception in a single feeling of love; here there is no distinction between barbarian and Greek, worthy and unworthy, friend and enemy, since all should be contemplated in God, not in themselves" (*Inst.* 2.8.55). Calvin based this belief on the fact that people are created in the image of God. He also invoked passages such as Galatians 3:28 ("There is no longer Jew or Greek, there is no longer slave or free, there is no longer male and female; for all of you are one in Christ Jesus"), which he believed made clear that one's value does not depend on religious, social, or gender status. Examples of Calvin's belief in equality were his advocacy of collegial ministry and his insistence that people who appeared before the consistory were supposed to receive equitable treatment no matter what their social station.

To his credit, Calvin was an opponent of slavery. He lived in a day of empire and colonization that brought with it a trafficking in human slaves. He argued that human beings were created free and equal, and that slavery, which is a result of sin, turns this freedom on its head. The New Testament, according to Calvin, opposes slavery, since a relationship with Christ abolishes distinctions of rank or privilege. Ever the realist, however, Calvin argued that where slavery persists, it should be regulated to lessen its evils.

Calvin wrote passionately about the importance of conscience and Christian liberty. This was most apparent in the first edition of the *Institutes*, written when the taste of persecution and exile were fresh in Calvin's mouth. In that edition, Calvin's concluding chapter on church and politics was set within a broader discussion of the priority of freedom. He argued that while people owe obedience to their rulers in the political realm, they should enjoy a certain measure of spiritual freedom within the church. They should adhere to the basics: obeying the Ten Commandments, believing the Apostles' Creed, and saying the Lord's Prayer. But beyond this, Christian consciences should not be unduly bound. The conscience should especially be free from customs and traditions with no clear mandate in Scripture.

To sum it up, as a child of his age Calvin could not have envisioned modern democracy with its separation of church and state. Yet many of his beliefs opened the door to a more revolutionary view of politics. He and his followers were active in the political arena, seeking to bend it toward God's will. This did not mean that Calvin naively thought government could fully remake the world. Calvin was no utopian. Moreover, he shared many of the blind spots of his age, as the burning of Servetus attests. Still, Calvin's affirmation of human equality is an important part of his legacy. Calvin expected believers not only to pray for God's will to be done but to actively work to make it so.

Economy and Society

We belong to God. We also belong to one another. As should be obvious, Calvin was concerned with the sanctification of the individual.

But he was just as focused on remaking the structures of society. Calvin's passion for social justice is visible throughout his writings.[3] Just as God is Lord of all, so Calvin fostered a vision of care for all. Calvin was adamant that one of the tests of a good society is whether and how it takes care of its poor.

As a refugee himself, Calvin had a special concern for the alien, the sojourner, and the stranger. In his biblical commentaries and in his pastoral practice, Calvin insisted that the privileged of the world needed to hear and respond to the cries of the wounded.

In keeping with this, Calvin took a number of steps to better the lives of the weak and disenfranchised. He established the office of deacon, which had the task of collecting and distributing monetary aid. In order to care for the influx of political refugees into Geneva, he created a social welfare fund, known as the *Bourse française*. In addition, he established a hospital. He founded the Geneva Academy for see for the education of the next generation, significantly including young girls.

On the economic front, Calvin spoke constantly in sermons and lectures about the proper use of money, and especially about the need for justice. He was concerned with just wages. His principles of moderation and stewardship aimed to guide the faithful toward an equitable way of living together.

Just as there has been debate over Calvin and democracy, a similar debate has raged over Calvin and capitalism. Early in the twentieth century, the sociologist Max Weber argued that Calvinism helped to produce the so-called Protestant work ethic, which in turn promoted the success of modern capitalism. By modern capitalism Weber meant an economy that employed modern financing techniques, cost accounting, the pursuit of profit, and the restriction of consumption.

Weber was not arguing that Calvinism somehow *caused* capitalism. Rather, his claim was that Calvinism, especially the Calvinism practiced by the Puritans, had what he called an "elective affinity" with capitalism. That is, it provided the fertile soil that helped capitalism grow. Weber asserted that Calvin's doctrine of election had the effect of making Calvinists perpetually nervous about the ultimate state of their souls. To compensate for this, the true Calvinist was driven to prove his or her election through action in the world. It is true that Calvinists have been active in the world, but Weber's psychological claims about the doctrine of election are difficult to substantiate.

More helpfully, Weber contrasted the "other-worldly" asceticism of the medieval world with the "inner-worldly" asceticism of Calvin. Asceticism is a form of self-denial. The medieval monk engaged in ascetic practices with a view toward storing up treasure in heaven. By contrast the Calvinist engaged in various forms of self-denial in living out God's calling in this world, here and now. Thus Calvinism produced a class of people who worked hard, saved, and were generous givers.

A practical example was the Calvinist attitude toward lending at interest. In the medieval world lending at interest, or usury, was forbidden to Christians and defined as a mortal sin. This was based on a certain reading of Luke 6:35: "But love your enemies, do good, and lend, expecting nothing in return." In the sixteenth century, Protestants argued that lending at interest was permitted as long as the terms were neither unfair nor oppressive nor violated charity between the parties. Calvin allowed lending at interest but subjected it to the standard of love. He also argued that the good to the community was a factor to take into account in judging particular forms of financing as good or bad.

Always Reforming: The Church Engages the World

Although for Calvin the institutions of this world (government, schools, the family) are ordained by God, this does not mean that we must simply accept them the way they are. Human beings are created to live in families, but in the twenty-first century there is diversity in what counts as a family. Human beings need to educate the young, but how they do this changes over time. Human beings need to govern themselves, but Calvin left leeway as to which form of government worked best in a given circumstance. Calvin would have had little patience with the ideological claim that a government governs best when it governs least. For Calvin a government governs best when it attends to the well-being of its people.

It is impossible to say what policy positions Calvin would favor in our complex twenty-first-century world. What we do know is that when Calvin gained sufficient influence he helped design a sewer system in Geneva. It is hard to imagine a Christian leader being more this-worldly than that. It may be true that some features of Calvin's theology, such as his support of private property and his openness to the charging of interest, contributed to the emergence of modern capitalism. But what is fairly certain is that Calvin would not have shrunk from offering a critique of the excesses to which capitalism is often prone. As I write this, the United States is in the throes of an acute credit crisis. Yet we are also captive to a more chronic economic condition. In a matter of a few decades the United States has evolved from a culture of thrift to a culture of conspicuous consumption and exponential debt. Such a development would have been unthinkable to Calvin.

Questions for Discussion

1. When has a change in your life given you new spiritual insights?
2. Name some ways that religious beliefs have public consequences. How are religious convictions shaping our social, political, and economic lives?
3. What do you make of the moral blind spots of Calvin, in the execution of Servetus, and of the pope who declared the St. Bartholomew's Day Massacre a cause for celebration? What lessons can we learn from this?
4. If, as Calvin maintained, one of the tests of a good society is how it takes care of its poor, then what grade does our American society receive? Are the poor only those who are economically disadvantaged? What can Christians do to minister to the poor in our society? What can your congregation do to minister to the poor in your midst?

Chapter 12

Reformed and Always Reforming

A premise of this book is that we have much to learn from Calvin. His powerful vision of a sovereign God who embraces our weakness in Jesus Christ, his unrelenting focus on hearing and rehearing the Word of God in Scripture, his conviction that the gospel includes the gift of Christian freedom, his passion for the transformation of social and political life—these features and more make his approach to the gospel worth exploring and amplifying.

At his own direction, Calvin's body was buried in an unmarked grave. Calvin had no intention of allowing the movement to which he had devoted his life to be turned into a cult of personality. Always wary of the human propensity to mingle religion and superstition, Calvin wanted to take no chance that his bones would become relics for future generations to venerate. By consigning his own body to obscurity, Calvin made clear that the church in Geneva was supposed to be following God, not John Calvin.

Yet to this day many people in the church seem to think that being "Reformed" is about agreeing to a list of things Calvin said five hundred years ago. Calvin would have been the first to reject this. His life of challenging the reigning religious powers of his day points us in the very opposite direction (chapter 1). For Calvin, the head of the church was none other than Jesus Christ. No human church leader, no hierarchical church structure, no confessional document, no list of essential tenets, no time-bound creed could claim this central position of authority. For Calvin, Christianity consisted of following the God who is *for* us by being *with* us in Jesus Christ and who is always at work *among* us by the power of the Holy Spirit. Being true to this

God requires a dynamic and self-critical theology, one that points beyond itself to the God who transcends human circumstance. This dynamism is visible in Calvin's treatment of each of the topics explored throughout the chapters of this book.

Reviewing Calvin's Approach to Theology

First, Calvin's doctrine of God illustrates his commitment to God's infinity and sovereign power at work in the world (chapter 2). God cannot be captured in a single system of thought—not Calvinism, not Lutheranism, not Roman Catholicism. There is always more to God than we can imagine or specify. This does not mean that we are consigned to silence about God, nor does it mean that we should abandon our Reformed convictions in frustration. But it does mean that following God is an Abrahamic journey that leads us to places we cannot always predict.

Second, Calvin's doctrine of grace challenges us to quit drawing lines in the sand when it comes to matters of Christian, Reformed, or Presbyterian orthodoxy (chapter 3). To require people to adhere to a set of essential tenets drawn from Calvin's writings is to ignore that we are justified (made right before God) not by the rectitude of our opinions but by the vitality of our relationship to God. The theology of *grace alone* carried with it for Calvin a powerful belief in freedom of conscience. This is one of many reasons that candidates for ordination in the Reformed faith are examined not on their ability to echo a list of propositions that other people believe. Rather, they are questioned concerning what *they* believe in the light of Scripture, under the guidance of the confessional heritage of the past, and in response to the present reality of God's grace. To organize church life around narrow doctrinal conformity is the antithesis of *grace alone*. In practice, Calvin pitched a big tent under which the family of Reformed churches could assemble, as his compromise with Bullinger on the sacraments attests (chapter 10).

Third, Calvin's doctrine of Scripture reminds us that the task of theological interpretation is never-ending. God's written Word brings us a divine message cloaked in human words (chapter 4). To put it another way, the infallible God used the words of fallible humans.

What could this mean except that God's truth cannot be contained in one set of writings or in the convictions of one group of people, one single church, or one nation or tribe? Look at the way Calvin makes a case for his own beliefs. He has no hesitation about quoting an ancient Greek philosopher when that supports his cause, because God can reveal God's own truth even through the mouths of non-Christians. But just as truth is not limited *to* Scripture, neither is error eliminated *from* Scripture. This is why Calvin never thinks twice about correcting occasional errors in the biblical tradition he inherited. Scripture presents us with a vast array of stories, symbols, and signs. These signs point us in many different directions, and they can mean many different things. Therefore, a biblical theologian is by definition an interpreter of the complexity of signs. Calvin himself was an expert interpreter. Sometimes he tried to harmonize and find unity in Scripture in ways that undercut the real diversity within the text. But again this only reminds us that our goal is not to repeat Calvin's interpretations but to equip ourselves to become as good at interpreting the Scriptures as he was.

Fourth, Calvin's doctrine of election reminds us that before we were, God was (chapter 5). God knows us, saves us, and equips us for service. Our lives are about embodying God's purposes, according to the unique set of gifts, insights, and passions God has given each of us. That is part of the reason for the rich diversity with which God has blessed us. What a bland and uninteresting world it would be if all of us thought and behaved like Calvin! In other words, the diversity that is everywhere evident in God's gracious election points to the need for a similar diversity in our theological reflection. The many insights that emerge from many diverse perspectives, temperaments, and places in time and space is one of God's amazing gifts to us.

Fifth, Calvin's doctrine of sin and salvation invests our theological reflection with a certain realism (chapter 6). We are all sinners who have fallen short of the glory of God. This is true of Calvin too. No one is good enough or wise enough to become the unquestioned authority over our spiritual lives. We need to be redeemed and restored to the image of God. This applies not only to our spiritual lives but to our theology as well. No theology ever gets it right. Every theology needs reforming and redeeming in accordance with the wisdom of Christ. As our prophet, Christ is the straightedge of truth against which our thoughts and deeds are to be measured. As our priest, Christ sacrifices his own life to put us in right relationship with God and one another. So too we must sacrifice our egos and our claims to certitude, and with humility be willing to receive correction in the light of Christ. As our king, Christ ushers us into his own new and better kingdom, where the power of grace and love supplant the exercise of raw political power and call us to a new way of living with our fellow human beings.

Sixth, just as we are justified (made right with God) by grace, so too we are sanctified (made holy) by grace (chapter 7). Calvin's doctrine of the Christian life points to an unfolding process of dying and rising, of giving up and taking on, of reaching in and reaching out in order to reach up. In other words, the Christian life involves both self denial and growth in grace. It is bursting with new life and unlimited in its possibilities. This is but another reason to embrace the ceaseless process of reform.

Seventh, Calvin's approach to the law and Christian ethics confirms the dynamism elsewhere visible in his theology (chapter 8). There is an overbearing tendency to elevate Calvin's theology, especially his doctrinal concepts, to a place of special privilege. But to take a set of Calvin's doctrinal concepts and freeze-frame them is to deny the dynamic quality of Christian living. Calvin did not preach and teach these doctrinal concepts for their own sakes. Biblical commentaries and sermons occupy a much greater portion of his literary output than his doctrinal writings. He was a pastor who was more practical than conceptual in his orientation. He cared what people thought because he knew that thoughts shape actions. If one's beliefs remained in one's head and never made it to the hands and feet, then Christian convictions would be nothing more than dead theology. In short, faith becomes evident in daily living; theology, for Calvin, was squarely oriented toward ethics.

Eighth, Calvin's doctrines of the church and its worship point to the need to find fresh ways to experience and praise God (chapters 9 and 10). Calvin spent much of his time reorganizing church life to meet the new demands of sixteenth-century culture. The same sort of effort is demanded today. The demise of Christendom suggests that doing business as usual in the church is not going to work. The challenge before the Western church is how to proclaim the gospel to coming generations in ways that are engaging, life-giving, and transformative. Just as Calvin advocated the innovation of putting the Psalter to music, so we may need to consider different forms of music in worship today. Just as Calvin reworked something as central to Christian identity and practice as the sacraments, so the church of the future may need to explore how the content of the sacraments can be further reformed in keeping with the gospel. The point is that for Calvin *content* took precedence over *form* in worship. Our focus should be the proclamation of the gospel in ways that are both faithful and creative.

Ninth, Calvin's perspectives on politics, economy, and society were similarly transformative (chapter 11). Calvin was seeking to bring every aspect of society under the lordship of Christ. To that end, Calvin challenged us to work toward creating communities where justice rolls down like waters and where citizens treat one another as bearers of the image of God. Calvin's emphasis on equality and his celebration of vocation may have had some indirect influence on the emergence of democracy, capitalism, and human rights. But it is also the case that Calvin did not always live up to his own best lights, as the burning of Servetus attests. If someone as principled and rigorous in his ethical standards as Calvin could commit such a glaring affront, then this should give every Christian pause. Calvin had unexamined assumptions that prevented him from living out the gospel fully and completely. So do we. Always being reformed means having the courage to "take every thought captive to obey Jesus Christ" (2 Cor. 10:5).

Always Reforming

New contexts require new measures of faithfulness in response to the ever-emerging reality of the gospel. This adaptability and attention to context has always been the strength of Reformed theological traditions. In 1934, hearing the Word of God afresh, Reformed Christians in Germany had the insight and the courage to resist Adolf Hitler through the witness of the Barmen Declaration, which boldly declared that "Jesus Christ, as he is attested for us in Holy Scripture, is the one Word of God which we have to hear and which we have to trust and obey in life and in death." Similarly, Reformed Christians in 1986 challenged apartheid in South Africa with the Belhar Confession, which spoke eloquently of the need for racial reconciliation. More recently, the World Alliance of Reformed Churches took a strong stand on the problem of global poverty and injustice in documents it released from its 24th General Council in Accra, Ghana, in 2004.[1]

As part of the 2004 Accra Council meeting, delegates visited Elmina and Cape Coast castles. Beginning in the seventeenth century, these castles were places where captured Africans were kept shackled before being shipped away and sold into slavery. When council delegates climbed up the steps of Elmina's women's dungeon, they emerged to discover a Reformed chapel, over whose entrance were inscribed the words: "The Lord has chosen Zion" (Ps. 132:13). Everyone was aghast. For two centuries, people who considered themselves among the Lord's "chosen" had worshiped and prayed in this space while directly beneath them human beings were chained in misery.

The delegates wondered aloud how the worshipers at Elmina, to whom they felt bound in a common profession of Christian and Reformed faith, could have been so spiritually and morally blind. On this trade in humans as commodities, wealth in Europe was built. Through their labor, sweat, suffering, intelligence, and creativity, the wealth of the Americas was developed.

How do God's people avoid this sort of blindness? How do we find the inspiration to live differently and to change what needs to be changed? The slave trade carried on from Elmina Castle provides agonizing proof that paying lip service to Calvin's doctrines in worship offers no guarantee that one is following the gospel in the real world.

The need for continual self-examination and reform is clear. This is the reason that many Reformed Christians have adopted the motto "the church reformed and always being reformed in accordance with the Word of God." The phrasing of this motto is instructive. It is not that the church decides for itself what reform entails; rather, the church is always in the process of *being* reformed as it responds to the dynamic voice of God's Word.

In the American context, Reformed Christians have responded to the Word through such actions as marching with Martin Luther King Jr., questioning the country's constant resort to war, searching for ways to alleviate poverty, and promoting stewardship of the planet.

Given this openness to discerning God's leading, it is no accident that some Reformed Christians were among the first to promote the ordination of women.

It is not the purpose of this book, or of this final chapter, to specify what the Reformed agenda should be for the present day. That is a task of discernment for which the whole church must take responsibility. It is a task that demands a reengagement with Scripture. It is also a task that invites us to pray. It is through the rhythms of prayer that we are able to distinguish the voice of God from all the other voices that vie for our attention. Prayer is always an action of first resort rather than last resort for Christian living, because it is intimate dialogue with God.

Calvin believed that our best model for prayer was the Lord's Prayer (Matt. 6:9–13; Luke 11:2–4), the prayer Jesus taught his disciples as a direct response to their request, "Lord, teach us to pray" (Luke 11:1). The Lord's Prayer was not a prayer intended to be memorized and repeated by rote. As Calvin observed, Jesus did not tell the disciples to repeat the particular words of the prayer but instead to "pray *in this manner*" (Matt. 6:9). The prayer that Jesus taught directs us to give attention first to the things of God, and then to the things that can distract us from loving and serving God and others. In short, this prayer echoes the two greatest commandments: love God and love your neighbor.

The Lord's Prayer has a definite structure. It begins with an invocation, a direct address of God ("Our Father in heaven"). That we pray to *our* Father gives us a vital clue to how we should think about life in connection to God. God's love and grace reach beyond a single nation, a single religious perspective, a single social or economic class, a single race or ethnicity, or a single gender or gender orientation. In Christ we believe that though these various features of our humanity may distinguish us, they need not divide us. We pray in solidarity with all people, and this gives us a benchmark for measuring what it means to be Reformed.

The opening invocation of the Lord's Prayer is then followed by a total of six petitions or requests made to God, the first three of which concern the glory of God: (1) "Hallowed be your name"; (2) "Your kingdom come"; and (3) "Your will be done, on earth as it is in heaven." The first petition operates like a cleansing breath. It invites us to focus on the majesty of God and to begin this prayer as it will end—with the awe of God. It is because of the excellence of God that God's name should be lifted up, that God should receive all praise, honor, and glory. The second petition ("Your kingdom come") is vital to Reformed identity, and it constitutes the thematic center of the prayer. Reformed Christians are a people who long for and work for the coming reign of God. Though God's reign is already breaking into the world, the Scriptures tell us that God's reign has not yet come in all its fullness. We pray for that fullness, and we seek to be a part of living into it. The third petition ("Your will be done, on earth as it is in heaven") is a direct continuation of this thought, reminding us that our faith in God is made real when we seek to bring heavenly commitments to fruition on earth.

The last three petitions pertain to our own specific human needs: (4) "Give us this day our daily bread"; (5) "And forgive us our debts, as we also have forgiven our debtors"; and (6) "do not bring us to the time of trial." The fourth petition ("Give us this day our daily bread") is vital to Reformed ethics. In one sense this petition has already been answered. The earth, which is God's good gift to us, already contains enough bounty to feed everyone. It is we who erect an obstacle to the petition's fulfillment. We are the ones who prevent the earth's abundance from being enjoyed by all. In the ancient world "bread" was a term used to mean "what it takes to live." That means that this request for daily bread is a broader request for the things that sustain life itself: food, clothing, shelter, health care, as well as the spiritual, emotional, and physical resources that bring general well-being for all people. To pray for daily bread is to acknowledge our identity as creatures in absolute dependence upon God; it is also to acknowledge our solidarity with others in need. No matter how rich or poor we are, it is only by God's daily grace that our daily needs are met.

The fifth petition ("And forgive us our debts, as we also have forgiven our debtors") goes to the heart of a Reformed view of community life. It is not by accident that the Apostles' Creed mentions the "forgiveness of sins" and the "communion of saints" in the same breath. True community is where true forgiveness is continually offered and received. It is when the church is bound together in a common life—or communion—of the Holy Spirit that this enactment of forgiveness is made possible. Hence these two things in the Lord's

Prayer are closely linked: the experience of being forgiven and extending forgiveness to others. This is a linkage that today's church, troubled by divisions and unrest, needs to reclaim.

The final petition ("Lead us not into temptation") asks God to help us not to succumb to evil. Acknowledging that God allows us to be tempted does not mean that God desires that we succumb to it. Rather, as with Jesus in the wilderness, times of temptation can cause us to depend anew on God, develop new strength of character, discover a clearer sense of direction, and learn to resist evil. This petition includes being saved from the temptations for which we are responsible, such as the temptation to deny the image of God in others by our heedless resort to coercion, exploitation, and violence. It also includes being saved from evils, whether those for which individuals are responsible or the larger, systemic evils surrounding us. This petition recognizes that we need God's power to deliver us from evil in all its forms.

Some manuscripts add a final doxology: "For the kingdom, and the power, and the glory are yours forever. Amen." Doxology, the giving of praise and honor and glory to God, is central to Calvin's vision of a Reformed church vitally engaged in the world. Relying on the power of God, we pray believing that, in the fullness of days, God will wipe every tear from our eyes, bind up every wound, and remove every obstacle that stands in the way of our redemption. Calvin's vision is one that looks with expectation toward the resurrection of the body and eternal life. As we seek to discern where God is leading us in the present day, Calvin would have us be mindful of the ways God has led us in the past. Although too often we have let our differences harden into division, we rejoice at the ways we have experienced God's faithfulness thus far. For it is God alone who calls and redeems us, corrects and forgives us, guides and equips us, to be a church reformed and always in the process of *being* reformed—in and for the twenty-first century.

Questions for Discussion

1. Name some things that you have learned from Calvin that positively inform your Christian faith.

2. What would you say to people who believe that good Reformed Christians are only those who agree with Calvin on most everything?

3. Calvin believed three things about Scripture that are held in tension: that truth is not limited to what we can find in Scripture; that the Scriptures contain factual errors; and that the Scriptures are the written Word of God. How can all of these positions be held simultaneously?

4. Calvin made major changes to the ways people worshiped. How threatening are innovations in worship in your congregation? Why? How might our Reformed heritage provide a way forward regarding new worship practices?

5. Is it possible to agree with Calvin's principles without coming to the same conclusions that he did? How might this work in the areas of election and predestination?

6. When Christians fight, split, and accuse one another of faithlessness, how does this affect the way the truth of the gospel is viewed by a watching world? Why do many Christian groups find it easier to split or splinter rather than adopt a position of mutual forbearance?

7. What does it mean to be reformed and always reforming?

Notes

CHAPTER 1: CALVIN: HIS LIFE AND INFLUENCE

1. For a list of books on Calvin's life, see the section "For Further Reading."

2. Calvin wrote about his expectations in a wife in a letter to Guillaume Farel, April 1539. *Corpus Reformatorum* 38, col. 340, translated in G. R. Potter and M. Greengrass, *John Calvin*, Documents of Modern History (New York: St. Martin's Press, 1983), 34.

CHAPTER 2: CALVIN'S VISION OF GOD

1. For the quotations from Habakkuk I am indebted to Nicholas Wolterstorff, "The Wounds of God. Calvin's Theology of Social Justice," *Reformed Journal* 37/6 (June 1987): 14–22; and to Dirk Smit, "Views on Calvin's Ethics: Reading Calvin in the South African Context,"*Reformed World* 57/4 (December 2007): 306–44.

2. For Calvin's approach to Trinitarian theology, see the excellent treatment by Philip Butin, *Revelation, Redemption, and Response: Calvin's Trinitarian Understanding of the Divine-Human Relationship* (Oxford: Oxford University Press, 1995).

3. One of the best treatments of the theme of "accommodation" in Calvin has been provided by David F. Wright, "Calvin's 'Accommodation' Revisited," in Peter De Klerk, ed., *Calvin as Exegete: Papers and Responses Presented at the Ninth Colloquium on Calvin and Calvin Studies, 1993* (Grand Rapids: CRC, 1995), 171–90; and Wright, "Calvin's Accommodating God," in *Calvinus Sincerioris Religionis Vindex: Calvin as Protector of the Purer Religion*, ed. Wilhelm H. Neuser and Brian G. Armstrong, 3–20 (Kirksville, MO: Sixteenth Century Journal Publications, 1997.

4. For a general treatment of Calvin on divine providence, see Susan E. Schreiner, *The Theater of His Glory: Nature and Its Natural Order in the Thought of John Calvin* (Durham, NC: Labyrinth Press, 1991).

CHAPTER 3: GRACE ALONE, CHRIST ALONE, FAITH ALONE

1. The medieval idea of "doing one's best" was summed up in a pithy Latin phrase, *facere quod in se est*. It means to do (*facere*) that which (*quod*) is in you (*in se est*). See Heiko A. Oberman, *The Harvest of Medieval Theology: Gabriel Biel and Late Medieval Nominalism* (Cambridge: Harvard University Press, 1963).

2. The idea that the divine Word is still free to rule the world even after having become incarnate in Jesus Christ came to be known as the "extra Calvinisticum," or the "extra" dimension in Calvin's thought. See Heiko Oberman, "The 'Extra' Dimension in the Theology of Calvin," *Journal of Ecclesiastical History* 21 (1970): 43–64; E. David Willis, *Calvin's Catholic Christology: The Function of the So-Called Extra Calvinisticum in Calvin's Theology* (Leiden: E. J. Brill, 1966).

3. Calvin's attempt at balance on the issue of justification and sanctification has caused one interpreter to label him a "crypto-Catholic." The claim is that Calvin did not adequately emphasize justification. Steven Ozment, *The Age of Reform: 1250–1550: An Intellectual and Religious History of Late Medieval and Reformation Europe* (New Haven: Yale University Press, 1980).

4. This is from the hymn "I Greet Thee, Who My Sure Redeemer Art," adapted from the Genevan Psalter, 1551. For the full text, see *The Presbyterian Hymnal: Hymns, Psalms, and Spiritual Songs* (Louisville: Westminster/John Knox Press, 1990), 457.

CHAPTER 4: WELLSPRING OF REFORM: SCRIPTURE ALONE

1. This way of formulating the issue emerged from a conversation with Jack Rogers in 1998.

2. This was a comment made by Luther at the Leipzig debate in 1519, quoted from Roland Bainton, *Here I Stand: A Life of Martin Luther* (Nashville: Abingdon Press, 1950), 117.

3. Calvin's approach to Scripture is treated in: Jack Forstman, *Word and Spirit: Calvin's Doctrine of Biblical Authority* (Stanford: Stanford University Press, 1962); John T. McNeill, "The Significance of the Word of God for Calvin," *Church History* 28 (1959): 131–46; Thomas F. Torrance, *The Hermeneutics of John Calvin*, Monograph Supplements to the *Scottish Journal of Theology* (Edinburgh: Scottish Academic Press, 1988). It is also useful to consider Calvin's exegesis of specific books of the Bible. See, for example, Susan E. Schreiner, *Where Shall Wisdom Be Found? Calvin's Exegesis of Job from Medieval and Modern Perspectives* (Chicago: University of Chicago Press, 1994); John L. Thompson, *John Calvin and the Daughters of Sarah: Women in Regular and Exceptional Roles in the Exegesis of Calvin, His Predecessors, and His Contemporaries*, Travaux d'Humanisme et Renaissance 259 (Geneva: Librairie Droz, 1992).

4. For an excellent account of Calvin and conscience, see Randall C. Zachman, *The Assurance of Faith: Conscience in the Theology of Martin Luther and John Calvin* (Minneapolis: Fortress Press, 1993).

CHAPTER 5: CHOSEN AND CALLED:
ELECTION AND PREDESTINATION

1. In addition to the writings of Calvin himself, I have been significantly influenced in the writing of this chapter by the reflections of Karl Barth in *Church Dogmatics* II/2.

2. Maya Angelou has made this comment in numerous interviews. See, for example, the one recorded by Teresa K. Weaver, Palm Beach Post-Cox News Service, Sunday, May 5, 2002, http://www.racematters.org/mayaangeloufinalchapter.htm. This comment may have inspired the erroneous claim that Maya Angelou wrote the poem "I Am a Christian," which actually was written by Carol Wimmer (see www.carolwimmer.com).

CHAPTER 6: THE WORKINGS OF SIN AND SALVATION

1. For Calvin on the will, see John H. Leith, "The Doctrine of the Will in the *Institutes of the Christian Religion*," in *Reformation Perennis: Essays on Calvin and the Reformation in Honor of Ford Lewis Battles*, ed. Brian A. Gerrish (Pittsburgh: Pickwick, 1981).

2. For Calvin's approach to the doctrine of humanity, see Mary Potter Engel, *John Calvin's Perspectival Anthropology* (Atlanta: Scholars Press, 1988).

3. For studies of Calvin's doctrine of Christ and salvation, see John F. Jansen, *Calvin's Doctrine of the Work of Christ* (London: James Clarke, 1985); and Paul van Buren, *Christ in Our Place: The Substitutionary Character of Calvin's Doctrine of Reconciliation* (Edinburgh: Oliver and Boyd, 1957).

CHAPTER 7: PARTICIPATION IN GOD'S WAYS:
THE POWER OF THE SPIRIT

1. For Calvin's theology of the Christian life, see John Leith, *John Calvin's Doctrine of the Christian Life* (Louisville: Westminster/John Knox, 1989); and Lucien Richard, *The Spirituality of John Calvin* (Atlanta: John Knox Press, 1974).

2. For an exploration of Calvin's teaching concerning things that do not matter, see Thomas Watson Street, "John Calvin on Adiaphora: An Exposition and Appraisal of His Theory and Practice," *Church History* 27, no. 1 (March 1958): 70–71.

CHAPTER 8: WHAT DOES GOD REQUIRE OF US?
LAW AND GOSPEL

1. In addition to Calvin's discussion of the Ten Commandments in the *Institutes*, see *John Calvin's Sermons on the Ten Commandments*, trans. Benjamin Wirt Farley (Grand Rapids: Baker, 1981). See also: Gunther H. Haas, *The Concept of Equity in Calvin's Ethics* (Waterloo, ON: Wilfred Laurier University Press, 1997); and I. John Hesselink, *Calvin's Concept of Law* (Allison Park, PA: Pickwick Publications, 1992).

2. H. Richard Niebuhr, *Radical Monotheism and Western Culture, with Supplementary Essays* (New York: Harper and Brothers, 1960).

CHAPTER 9: THE CHURCH:
MEANING, MINISTRY AND MISSION

1. This discussion is influenced, in part, by the Reformed theologian Heinrich Bullinger, who argued that the Reformed faith should also be "authentic" (i.e., evangelical), "catholic," and "orthodox." See *The Decades of Henry Bullinger*, ed. Thomas Harding, 5 vols. (Cambridge: Cambridge University Press, 1849), 1:45.

2. For more on the ministry, see Elsie Anne McKee, *John Calvin on the Diaconate and Liturgical Almsgiving* (Geneva: Librairie Droz, 1984); idem, *Diakonia in the Classical Reformed Tradition and Today* (Grand Rapids: Wm. B. Eerdmans, 1989).

CHAPTER 10: CONNECTING TO GOD:
WORSHIP AND SACRAMENTS

1. For more on Calvin as a preacher, see Hughes Oliphant Old, *The Reading and Preaching of the Scriptures in the Worship of the Christian Church*, vol. 4, *The Age of the Reformation* (Grand Rapids: Eerdmans, 2002); Ronald S. Wallace, *Calvin's Doctrine of the Word and Sacrament* (Edinburgh: Oliver and Boyd, 1953).

2. For introductions to Calvin's doctrine of the sacraments, see: Brian Gerrish, *Grace and Gratitude: The Eucharistic Theology of John Calvin* (Minneapolis: Fortress Press, 1993); Killian McDonnell, *John Calvin, the Church, and the Eucharist* (Princeton: Princeton University Press, 1967).

3. For more on the importance of the agreement between Calvin and Bullinger on the Lord's Supper, see the following incisive works: Timothy George, "John Calvin and the Agreement of Zurich (1549)," in *John Calvin and the Church: A Prism of Reform*, ed. Timothy George (Louisville: Westminster/John Knox Press, 1990); Paul Rorem, *Calvin and Bullinger on the Lord's Supper* (Bramcote: Grove Books Limited, 1989); idem, "The Consensus Tigurinus (1549): Did Calvin Compromise?" in *Calvinus Sacrae Scripturae Professor*, edited by Wilhelm H. Neuser (Grand Rapids: Eerdmans, 1994), 72–90.

CHAPTER 11: POLITICS, ECONOMY, AND SOCIETY

1. See the section "For Further Reading" for books on Calvin and politics. The interpretation of Calvin I adopt puts me at odds with those who see little relationship between Calvin and democracy, as well as those who claim that Calvin's views were mostly dependent on Luther. For an example of the former, see George H. Sabine and Thomas L. Thorson, *A History of Political Theory*, 4th edition (New York: Rinehart and Winston, 1973), 340–43. For an example of the latter, see Quentin Skinner, *The Foundations of Modern Political Thought* (Cambridge: Cambridge University Press, 1978), vol. 1, chs. 1–2.

2. See Roland H. Bainton, *Hunted Heretic: The Life and Death of Michael Servetus, 1511–1553* (Boston: The Beacon Press, 1953).

3. See the section "For Further Reading" for books on Calvin and economy, society, and culture.

CHAPTER 12: REFORMED AND ALWAYS REFORMING

1. The Barmen Declaration (1934), the Belhar Confession (1984), and the Letter from Accra (2004) are all available from the Web site of the World Alliance of Reformed Churches, http://warc.jalb.de/warcajsp/side.jsp?news_id=157&navi=1.

Glossary

Accommodation—the idea that the infinite God reveals to us who God is in ways that finite humans can understand. Human parents do this same translation process as they communicate with their children of various ages and abilities.

Adoption—a teaching found in a number of places in the New Testament that believers, through their union with Christ by the Spirit's power, have become children of God (Rom. 8:15, 23; 9:4; Gal. 4:5; Eph. 1:5; John 1:12).

Antinomianism—the false belief that for those who are in Christ, God has completely done away with the obligation to follow the law.

Apostolic—having to do with the first apostles; in reference to the church, Calvin insisted that the church is apostolic not because of an uninterrupted leadership chain reaching from Peter forward, but rather that the church is apostolic when it follows the teaching of the apostles as witnessed in Scripture.

Apostolic succession—the claim of the Roman Catholic Church that the pope is part of an uninterrupted leadership chain reaching from Peter forward to the present.

Asceticism—a lifestyle marked by self-denial, usually with a spiritual purpose.

Catholic—(with a lower-case *c*)—in reference to the church, it means that there is a single church that is universal, not limited to one location in time or space.

Cheap grace—taking God's gracious offer of forgiveness in Christ lightly; assuming freedom from the guilt of sin without genuine repentance for sin.

Christendom—a coherent Christian civilization where everything in the broader culture works to support the existence of the church. Rulers of the world are expected to protect and defend the cause of Christ, while the church is expected to provide the moral values for the citizenry.

Church fathers—widely respected spiritual leaders in the early church such as Irenaeus, Athanasius, and Cyril in the East, and Augustine, Anselm, and Thomas Aquinas in the West.

Consistory—created by Calvin in 1542, this was a governing council for the city composed of both clergy and lay elders that dealt primarily with matters of behavior, including non-Reformed religious practices, financial disputes, marital strife, sexual infidelity, and personal conflicts of various sorts.

Council of Chalcedon (451 CE)—declared that Jesus Christ is both fully human and fully divine.

Council of Nicaea (325 CE)—declared that Jesus and God are of the same reality; that God in Christ assumes our human nature and becomes one with us.

Double grace—the first form of grace is the grace by which we are reckoned righteous once and for all (justification); the second form is the grace by which we are increasingly made righteous over time (sanctification).

Double predestination—a belief that Calvin took from Augustine and modified that before the foundation of the world God ordained some people to eternal life and others to eternal damnation.

Election—the biblical belief that prior to any human action or merit, God chooses certain people with whom to have a special relationship, and through whom to work out divine purposes for the benefit of the whole world.

Excommunication—a form of church discipline whereby a church member is refused the sacrament of Holy Communion. This form of punishment is public and hence humiliating.

Fatalism—the view that whatever happens is bound to happen, and neither God nor human beings can change fate's course.

First table of the Ten Commandments—commandments 1–4, having to do with one's duty to God.

Forensic view of justification—God's gracious declaration of "not guilty" on humans who most certainly *are* guilty of sin.

Grace—God's favor, bestowed without regard to human merit.

Historical providence—the belief that God is at work in history, in culture, and in the workings of society to bend the will of humans to serve divine goodness.

Imparted righteousness—a Roman Catholic teaching that says that in Christ there is an immediate righteousness or change in status that becomes the ground of our reconciliation with God. Calvin objected to the notion that there was some kind of righteousness that was an indelible, inherent, or integral part of our human fabric.

Imputed righteousness—the "not guilty" status of Christ that is attributed to us by God even though we are guilty of sin.

Irresistible grace—the belief that God's grace cannot be resisted by the human will.

Justification (making us right)—the forgiveness of Christ that puts one in a right relationship with God; the act of God's free grace by which we are accepted as righteous in God's sight based on the righteousness of Christ being attributed to us. *See also* **Sanctification.**

Limited atonement—Christ's death is salvific only for the elect.

Marks of the true church—hallmarks that distinguish a true church from a false one. Calvin lifted up two marks: where the Word is rightly preached and where the sacraments are rightly administered. Some Reformed confessions added a third mark: administration of church discipline. There is even some indication of a fourth mark: almsgiving.

Means of grace—a vehicle for the grace and goodness of God to be expressed to humans. Calvin referred to the church and the sacraments as means of grace.

Mortification—the sorrow of soul that comes from the recognition and acknowledgment of the bad things one has done; a putting to death of sinful ways of life in order to begin to live for God and neighbor.

Original righteousness—the sinless state that Adam and Eve enjoyed before the fall.

Original sin—the sin of Adam and Eve whereby original righteousness was lost forever.

Orthodox—literally, "right opinion." Used in reference to theology, it means right opinions about God, the Bible, or the Christian faith and practice. The word is also used in reference to the Greek, Russian, and Syrian Orthodox Churches.

Perseverance of the saints—the belief that the power of God will ensure that the elect are saved. The motto form of this is, "once saved, always saved."

Predestination—the belief that God has given humanity a heavenly destiny, a future that God alone secures. Predestination teaches that God does not create us and then abandon us to our own devices. Instead, God guides the elect in ways that allow the exercise of human free will, while also enabling the faithful to move reliably toward a heavenly destiny.

Predeterminism—the idea, often mistaken for predestination, that God has already orchestrated every event in our future, eliminating our ability to choose our own actions.

Priesthood of all believers—the spiritual equality of all Christians before God; shared leadership in the church between clergy and laity.

Reformed—the word literally means to refashion or render something anew. Calvin believed that the church always needs self-critique, an ongoing reexamination of every area of its life in the light of the Scriptures.

Reformed tradition—the beliefs, practices, and ways of understanding Scripture that are the foundation for a Protestant critique of Roman Catholicism.

Reformers—those who wanted to see the structure, worship, practices, and leadership of the Roman Catholic Church reshaped.

Regeneration—the act of God's grace whereby we are enabled to die unto sin, live unto righteousness, and be renewed in the image of Jesus Christ.

Repentance—the true turning of our life to God, a turning that arises from a pure and earnest fear of God; it consists in the mortification of our flesh and of the old person, and in the vivification of the Spirit.

Reprobate—those who are unsaved.

Righteousness of God—God's absolute trustworthiness in fulfilling divine promises.

Sacrament—according to Augustine a sacrament is an outward and visible sign of an inward and spiritual grace. Calvin insisted that sacraments be firmly connected to the promises and commandments of Christ. Calvin recognized only baptism and the Lord's Supper as true sacraments of the church.

Sanctification (making us holy)—the spiritual growth that occurs as a result of union with Christ; the act of God's free grace by which we are regenerated, enabled to die unto sin, live unto righteousness, and be renewed in the image of Jesus Christ. *See also* **Justification**.

Second table of the Ten Commandments—commandments 5–10, having to do with one's duty to fellow humans.

Sense of divinity—an innate awareness of God's presence in one's life. Calvin believed that all people have this basic awareness.

Servetus—Michael Servetus (b. 1511) was a Spanish physician who was considered a heretic by both Catholics and Protestants. He denied the doctrine of the Trinity and objected to infant baptism. After a dramatic trial in Geneva, he was burned at the stake on October 27, 1553.

Sovereignty—a word from the political realm that connotes the possession and exercise of supreme political power. It is often used to describe the power of God. Though Calvin is credited with championing the sovereignty of God, the term never appears in the *Institutes.*

Special providence—the teaching that God is especially at work in the lives of the faithful.

Theocracy—a form of government in which religious powers rule civil affairs.

Total depravity—the belief taught by those who came after Calvin that human beings are so sinful that we are incapable of contributing anything to our own salvation, including good works.

Transubstantiation—the idea that the elements of bread and wine are transformed into the actual body and blood of Jesus Christ by the words of institution spoken by a Roman Catholic priest during a Mass.

Unconditional election—the belief that God's selection of humans for salvation does not base itself on any human response, including having a prior faith in Jesus Christ.

Universal providence—the order and rhythms of nature that govern all creation.

Vivification—living unto righteousness; coming alive to Christ in the power of the Spirit; living in a manner pleasing to God.

Zurich Consent (*Consensus Tigurinus*)—a compromise statement forged by Calvin (Geneva) and Heinrich Bullinger (Zurich) in 1549 that paved the way for a common Reformed theology. They agreed that the sacraments serve to lead believers to Christ, are secondary to the gospel, facilitate union with Christ, and are a public, communal celebration that deepens the faith of the whole community, and that in the sacrament there is real movement both from God to us and from us to God. They also agreed that the sacrament does not have the power in itself to convey salvation.

For Further Reading

A number of excellent resources on the life of Calvin are available, among them:

Bouwsma, William J. *John Calvin: A Sixteenth-Century Portrait.* New York: Oxford University Press, 1988.

Cottret, Bernard. *Calvin: A Biography.* Trans. M. Wallace McDonald. Grand Rapids: Eerdmans, 2000.

Ganoczy, Alexandre. *The Young Calvin.* Trans. David L. Foxgrover and Wade Provo. Philadelphia: Westminster Press, 1987.

McGrath, Alister. *A Life of John Calvin.* Oxford: Blackwell, 1990.

McNeill, John T. *The History and Character of Calvinism.* New York: Oxford University Press, 1954.

Parker, T. H. L. *John Calvin: A Biography.* Louisville: Westminster John Knox Press, 2007.

Potter, G. R., and M. Greengrass. *John Calvin.* Documents in Modern History. New York: St. Martins Press, 1983.

For general introductions to Calvin's theology, see the following:

Dowey, Edward A., Jr. *The Knowledge of God in Calvin's Theology.* New York: Columbia University Press, 1952.

Hesselink, I. John. *Calvin's First Cathechism: A Commentary.* Louisville: Westminster John Knox Press, 1997.

Jones, Serene. *Calvin and the Rhetoric of Piety.* Louisville: Westminster John Knox Press, 1995.

McKim, Donald K., ed. *The Cambridge Companion to John Calvin.* New York: Cambridge University Press, 2004.

Partee, Charles. *The Theology of John Calvin.* Louisville: Westminster John Knox Press, 2008.

Wendel, François. *Calvin: The Origins and Development of His Thought.* Durham, NC: Labyrinth Press, 1995.

For Calvin on politics, see:

Beza, Theodore. *Concerning the Rights of Rulers over Their Subjects and the Duty of Subjects towards Their Rulers*. Trans. Henri-Louis Gonin. Capetown, Pretoria: H.A.U.M., 1956.

Hancock, Ralph C. *Calvin and the Foundations of Modern Politics*. Ithaca: Cornell, 1989.

Höpfl, Harro. *The Christian Polity of John Calvin*. Cambridge Studies in the History and Theory of Politics. New York: Cambridge University Press, 1982.

Little, David. *Religion, Order, and Law: A Study in Pre-Revolutionary England*. New York: Harper & Row, 1969.

Skinner, Quentin. *The Foundations of Modern Political Thought*. 2 vols. Cambridge: Cambridge University Press, 1978.

Waltzer, Michael. *The Revolution of the Saints*. Cambridge, MA: Harvard University Press, 1965.

For Calvin on economy, society, and culture, see:

Biéler, André. *Calvin's Economic and Social Thought*. Trans. James Greig. Geneva: World Council of Churches, 2005.

Douglass, Jane Dempsey. *Women, Freedom, and Calvin*. Philadelphia: Westminster Press, 1985.

Graham, W. Fred. *The Constructive Revolutionary: John Calvin and His Socio-Economic Impact*. East Lansing: Michigan State University Press, 1987.

Olson, Jeannine. *Calvin and Social Welfare: Deacons and the Bourse française*. Selinsgrove: Susquehanna University Press, 1989.

Tawney, R. H. *Religion and the Rise of Capitalism*. New York: Harcourt Brace & World, 1926.

Troeltsch, Ernst. *The Social Teachings of the Christian Churches*. Trans. Olive Wyon. 2 vols. New York: Macmillan, 1931.

Weber, Max. *The Protestant Ethic and the Spirit of Capitalism: The Relation between Religion and the Economic and Social Life of Modern Culture*. Trans. Talcot Parsons. New York: Scribners, 1958.